THIS BOOK IS

DEDICATED

TO KEN FANTI

Who always hid my keys, my wallet,
and my phone

but never my heart. A better friend
you cannot find.

(He's sleeping while watching TV)

TABLE OF

CONTENTS

....

CHAPTER 1

MONEY THE EASY WAY

 Money is not hard to obtain, hanging on to it is the key. My whole life I have had to support myself. My father, because he had to work on his parent's farm, only had a 5th grade education. When he was older, he worked in the construction field which would have been fine but he became an alcoholic. He was a hardworking man and believed in putting 110% in everything he did but in the evening the other guys on the job would say; "Hey Jack, let's go and get a beer" , problem was, he didn't know when to quit. He wasn't bad to me or my mother and in later years, he finally realized that he couldn't take even one drink and stayed away from alcohol but once in a

while he would go off the deep end. My mother worked a regular job to put food on the table and this was back when women stayed home. In the earlier years, my dad would spend or lose his whole paycheck and my mom's pay was all we lived on. When I was growing up in the Portland, Oregon area, I went to 22 grade schools from the 3rd grade thru the 8th grade and went to 3 different high schools before graduating. It would have been more but I went to an "all boy's" technical high school, "Benson". I could go to Benson H.S. and live anywhere in the city as long as I maintained above average grades. It was there where I got most of my skills for life's work place like mechanical drawing, electricity, sheet metal, automotive, electronics, wood shop, welding, and aviation dynamics. Unfortunately, we moved out into the suburbs for my last 2 years of school and I ended up going to 2 other high schools before graduating.

As a teenager, every summer, for as long as I could remember, I picked strawberries, raspberries, and beans to pay for my school clothes, supplies etc. I guess that is what started me on the road to becoming a

work-a-holic, seeing that I could take care of my needs if I just applied myself.

Right after I got out of the Navy in Chicago, I met my wonderful wife. And to keep her home so she could raise our 2 boys, I had, at one time, 7 part-time jobs until I got smart and started my own janitorial business. I had 11 employees working during the daytime with residential cleaning and at nite with commercial cleaning. Most of my workers were college students from Northwestern University (an Ivy League college). I asked them what they wanted to be when they grew –up and they would tell me; "a professional college student". You see, as long as their parents paid their way, why should they quit school.

My janitorial business was growing and in 1973, I had the regional office of the largest mailing machine company in the United States, Pitney Bowes. I was starting to bid on big companies like Max Factor. I was on my way up. The name of my business was called:

The Sponge – "We absorb your cleaning problems"

It wasn't the name that got me the business, although it was cute in the beginning but towards the end the name was kind of silly. No, it was the area prefix on my phone. My area prefix was 256 and everyone in Chicago knew that was the upper North Shore where the rich lived. But we fooled them; we lived on the other side of the tracks (the poor side of the North Shore). Everything was just like peas and carrots until my wife and I got a divorce (I was always working and never home). There went the business. I gave it away to the employees. It was either giving my ex-wife 75% of the gross profits from the business (what with her having the 2 boys and all) or selling the business and giving her 75% of the sale.

Looking back, what I should have done, I should have given her the 75% of the gross profit at the time and kept my janitorial business, hassling for more business until I was back on top again.

Money is easy to obtain but it is hard to hang on to.

CHAPTER 2

GUIDELINES

DO'S/DON'TS

Here are 6 guidelines that the other guys tell you to watch for when you're starting a business for yourself.

#1-Pick a business that is not limited to age, race or sex.

There are right. When you limit your business to, let say Senior Citizens, you are also limiting your income. And that is OK if you have a big variety to choose from like AARP.

#2-Pick a business that you are familiar with.

Well yah, that's right. I'll get into it later but if you know what you are doing you don't have to know the business that well but your employees do. Like I said, I'll get into it, more in length, later on.

#3-If you have a great idea don't let anyone talk you out of it.

Boy is that true. People will always try to talk you out of owning your own business especially a spouse. "Owning your own business is not as secure as a weekly paycheck". That's what they will tell you. WRONG – You will make at least 5 times more money owning your own business than collecting a weekly paycheck. And if you stay on top of your business you shouldn't have to worries about security. By the way, there is NO weekly paycheck job that is secure, NO NOT ONE. It is good to talk in general about your business to some good friends; they might give you some good insight. But if you really have an **"Itch"** for having your own business then someday you will need to scratch that "itch" or you will go nuts and you will drive everyone around you nuts too.

#4-Have about 3 months start-up capital.

That is very true. That 3 months start-up money will probably turn into 2 months start-up money because there is always something that comes up that you didn't plan on in the beginning.

#5-75% of most businesses fail in the first 3 to 5 years.

THATS A CROCK 75% of most marriages fail in the first 3 to 5 years. 75% of most BUSINESSES fail in the first 3 MONTHS. Most people start up a business not knowing what they are doing or where they are going. They never took the time to plan ahead. If you are walking along a path shouldn't you make sure that the path ahead has no quicksand? Thank You! This is one of the reasons why I am writing this book so you don't fall into quicksand.

A dear friend of mine had a real good computer recycling business. What this type of business does is to pick-up old computers. If the computer could be refurbished, that was icing on the cake but if not, then the computer would be broken down for scrap and sent to China for destroying. My job was being his bookkeeper and tax consultant at the time. He wanted to expand his business with over-the-road trucks (A great idea but risky and complicated). My friend knew a lot about computers but knew less than nothing about trucks or truck driving. And the problem was he didn't want to listen to sound ideas from his staff to make it work. He went ahead on his own and 6 months later he lost his computer business, his house, his cars and almost his wife. The _good drivers_ were ripping him off. And the inexperience drivers were ruining his trucks plus the cargo inside.

Don't say this will never happen to you because you're too smart for that. My friend was and still is, one of the smartest men I have ever known, he just made a poor judgment call.

I had a painting business at one time and I needed a gofer (go for this, go for that). I was spray painting inside and I guess I made it look too easy because this kid I hired (a gofer and "warm body") who had no experience at all in the painting business, said to me; "When I get my inheritance, I am going to buy my own spray paint rig and start my own painting business". Don't make the wrong judgment call. Get some good sound advice and listen to it. All large companies and including being the Presidents of the United States have advisers (hopefully good ones and hopefully they listen to them).

#6-Don't hire relatives or friends.

Sound advice, a relative or friend will rip you off in a heartbeat. Or how about if they don't do the work you ask of them or if they mess-up the work, how are you going to fire them? They are your relative or friend so they <u>have a right</u> to be late or even lazy, right! Or maybe they want to tell you how to run the business. Oh! And in about <u>3 days of working for you,</u> they will be asking you for a raise. You can avoid all this by not hiring your friends or relatives.

Asking for a raise --- I remember this guy from my "experienced painter" ad who called me up and asked for a job. I said to him; "Come down to the job site and fill out the paperwork". After not finding the place which was 1 block off a major street, the next day he calls me up for directions again and asked me if he could get a dollar more an hour. I said to him; "You couldn't find the place which was easy to find, I haven't seen you or even hired you yet nor do I even know if you are qualified for the job and you want a raise (as I'm falling down lol)"
"Most people want the money but few are willing to work for it." Sad but true.

Here are a few more Do's and DON'Ts to follow that they forgot to tell you.

#1-Don't pick a bad names for your company.

You want a name that is easy to pronounce and to remember. A name; that rolls-off-the-tongue and one that isn't too long to write on a check. Your last name should be avoided at all cost. Some Jews don't like Germans and some Germans don't like Jews.

Ever Bank bought the Jacksonville Stadium and renamed the stadium Ever Bank. I guess that isn't too bad but how about Fifth Third Bank? Have you ever been behind a car with personalized plates that only make sense to them? Kind of like Fifth Third Bank. How about; "Joe's Pizza and Hot Buffalo Wings Emporium" (too long for a check)? Oh! And "The Sponge" (my business), it may sound cute for a janitorial business but it wasn't business-like.

#2-Don't buy, when you are starting up a business, a lot of supplies and things you may not need right away.

Keep your expenses to a minimum. Wait until you have some profit to buy those 5 computers that are on sale now but you only need one. Believe me, whatever it is, will be on sale again later no matter what they tell you. TRUST ME.

#3-Don't spend a lot of money on advertising.

Like the "Yellow Pages" they are great but in the beginning that kind of investment could ruin you before you get started. I will show you later how much, if any, money you should invest to get your business off the ground.

#4-Don't give your customer such a deal that you go in the hole and not make enough money to pay for your expenses.

I worked for this other recycling computer firm as a truck driver. We would go 200 miles to pick-up a 1,000 pounds of scrap (old computers and printers). The problem was he would make 3 cents a pound profit (about $30.00) and spend $120.00 for gas (5 miles to the gallon = 40 gallons X $3.00 per gallon) plus our wages. The owner's reasoning was, "The customer will give us more business in the future". In the future, that same customer gave us the same amount of business and we lost money again.

#5-Do plan on spending at least 10 to 12 hours a day to get your business going.

Someone else is probably not going to make your business a success, like <u>you</u> will. National average has most successful business owners working a minimum of 10 to 14 hours a day. <u>Plan on it!</u>

#6-Do make complete plans on how you are going to start the business and what capital (money) you will need for 3 months.

This is so important I probably should have put it in giant letters. If you never had a budget before, plan for it now. You should write down everything from not only equipment and supplies but also the gas that it is going to take to get those supplies and equipment. How you advertising and whither you need a computer, printer, business cards, uniforms, business phone, ink for the printer, paper for the printer, envelopes, stamps, and how about a

P.O. Box. Your car is a factor just getting to P.O. and the job site. Do you need to make any arrangements with spouse, friends or customers that might eat up gas and/or time? YOU need to plan every single moment and every amount of money that will be needed. If you are thinking that this is STUPID, think again. It just might be the difference of making it without pulling out your hair or borrowing money that you don't have.

#7-Don't use your home address, phone #, or name.

This will save you a ton of headaches down the road.

Instead of using your address in the advertisement, get a P.O. Box with an address. UPS stores have them.

Phone # is OK if the business volume is small but once your business takes off, the volume maybe more than you want to handle. Have an answering service or give them your e-mail address.

Your full name given out to people you haven't even met is <u>too personal</u>. If you must use your name, give them your first name or your last name only, PERIOD.

#8-Don't move too fast.

Listen, I know you want get out there and win the world with you talent, your wit, and your charm but common sense is the key. Don't go after the "Big Dogs" until you have biting experience. Stay small if you get bit you can lick your wounds. Wait until you have the experience and you can't stand being small anymore.

Big Dogs know other big dogs but they don't know and don't care about little puppies. Big Dogs eat little puppies for lunch. And you may not recover from such a sacrifice.

I had an office on a major street for doing taxes. Plus I had 30 years of experience behind me. But I was small potatoes next to H & R Block. The edge I had over them and others was <u>NO WAITING LINES</u>, service was <u>½ THE PRICE</u>, and I gave <u>QUOTES OVER THE PHONE</u>.

I had a millionaire lady who came to me because she didn't want to pay CPA prices nor did she want to wait in long lines like at H & R Block. I have been doing her taxes and bookkeeping for the past 10 years now.

#9-Make plans for your bookkeeping and taxes.

NEVER FEAR

I have included a couple of chapters for you, LATER.

When I first started my Janitorial Service I trusted someone to take care of my taxes. The following year I was audited at my office by the **IRS**. I was sweating bullets. The end result was a payback of $2,000 to the IRS. That was in the early 70's today that money would feel like $20,000. I did my own taxes after that ordeal.

#10-Think outside the box.

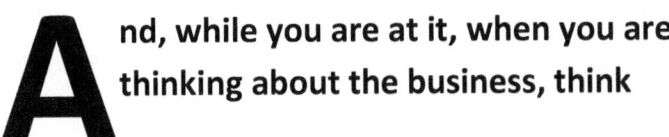 **A**nd, while you are at it, when you are thinking about the business, think

"outside the box". Another words, give your business a new wrinkle.

With my bookkeeping business, I had a paperless bookkeeping system for my customers. They would put all of their income (bank deposit slips) and expense receipts in a bag that I provided them with my phone # on it just in case the bag ever was lost. They NEVER had to see those receipts again. At the end of the month, I would replace the full bag with an empty one.

Just remember, you are probably not the first person to think of the business nor are you the only one out there working it. Stay ahead of the competition and think "outside the box" ......they are.

CHAPTER 3

100

BUSINESSES

YOU CAN START

WITH LITTLE OR

NO MONEY

1 – RESIDENTIAL CLEANING SERVICE

Bring in a crew, a vacuum, and some cleaning supplies to get started running (in my business, I bought restored Electrolux machines. They are sturdy with strong pull-pounds and they don't need a rotating brush).

When you are picking a crew, screen them first. After all, you don't want them to steal from your customers. Before you start the work, you will need to know what the customer wants done and <u>you set</u> what the job is going to pay. It would be good to have a written contract with all the work and pay spelled out for the customer to sign, so no problems will arise when you do get paid. Unfortunately, even if you are doing this job for a friend, have a contract. <u>No exceptions</u>. By the way, you will NEVER be able to collect your money in a court of law without a contract.

Set-up with the customer (in the contract) the amount of times your company will do the cleaning each month.

I would set-up a "one time" job first. Saying to the customer, "Some of the work here needs to be done one time before we can start cleaning on a regular basis." This way I could pay for my supplies plus the customers like it when you treated their house special. Just don't go overboard. Also give your company business a name and don't forget to have some business cards made up. Start with friends or advertise on Craigslist.

2-MAID SERVICE RESIDENTIAL CLEANING

Dress your crew in maid outfits (preferably women). The best advertisement for this work would probably be a colorful advertising magazine with a coupon saying 10% off for the first time service. You still need to screen your workers. By the way, you should be there with your workers to make sure that the work goes fast, organized and that all the work gets done that is on the contract. Another reason for you to be there is so no "hanky-panky" goes on between the maids (in their uniforms) and the customer you're doing the work for. In Maid Service Residential Cleaning the customer should have all the supplies. You also need to get your name out there quickly. Most customers are going to want your company to have good references before they let you in the door. With a maid service company, springing for some snappy uniforms is a must. You need to find a way to beat out the companion. You should be able to find a rental and/or laundry service. <u>Don't</u> get skimpy sexy uniforms. Have the employees be around the same size. The employees should be pleasing to the eye and courteous (yes mama and yes sir) to the customer and their guests. If you make a good impression then your company shouldn't have any problems getting references. And guess what? When you have good references your money starts rolling in. Soon after that you should be able to raise your prices just a little. It is called <u>Supply and Demand</u>.

3- MAID REFERRAL SERVICE

This is a great service if you don't want to do more then put your feet up and answer the phone. Of course, we know there is more to the service then that. First again, you will need to screen the people you send out to the  customers. And you will need to provide or have the employees provide their own uniforms. I like the employee providing their own uniforms and have them clean the uniform as well. You start out by taking applications for your service. Do background checks with experience checks as well. Then tell the applicant that you will call them when a job comes up. A good means of advertising for this service would be using a magazine mailer for customers. When you get a customer ask them what they want done and explain the payment arrangement. After a date and time is set call the applicant and give them the address with directions and when they are to be at the customer's house. Make sure the applicant knows to be there on time or a little before. <u>Never be late.</u> The money arrangement should be with you and the customer. Never have the customer give the money to the applicant unless you know that the applicant will give the money to you. There is a "sweet" way to have the customer give the money to the applicant. It is explained in 100 Businesses under Student Cleaning Service.

4 – BUTLER REFERRAL SERVICE

_Make sure your people are screened completely more than you would for a

maid service. Understand, a butler is usually in charge over the entire staff including the maids, the cooks, the gardener, the chauffeur etc. Your butler applicant should have references dating back 3 to 5 years.

5 – COMMERCIAL JANITORIAL SERVICE

This is a great business to have little or no experience and very little upfront cash to start. The best way to find clients is the buy a mailing list of commercial companies. 20% maybe old useless addresses but it is the fastest way to get a mailing list with zip codes.

When starting a commercial janitorial service you have to get your business name out there to the owner or boss of the company. But it is

impossible to get past the secretary who is usually clueless to the financial status of her company or whether the owner wants to use a janitorial service or change the one they might be using now. And for the most part she won't bother her boss to find out. So you knocking on her door will only get your business card the deep 6. She doesn't have the time nor does she understand what you are trying to tell her about your business and the needs of her boss. Send the company a letter. The secretary will open it along with all the other mail she gets and will see that you are a janitorial business and pass it on to the boss. Or if she has time, she will be nosey and read your business letter and decide on her own whether "her company" needs you or not. Deep 6 will probably be the answer. If or when you get passed her and into the hands of the owner, he can make the decision as to whether to call you or not. By the way, you don't have to spend a lot of money on your letter, just list the work you do (in black ink, no color) and thank him for his time.

During the appointment, check over his place and let him know that you will have to do a 1 time job first to get the place up to your standard before you start the normal routine. This way you can get some money up front to buy the supplies and equipment you will need to do his company on a routine bases. A few pieces of equipment, like a striping machine maybe needed for his company (don't buy new – too costly, buy one on Craigslist), vacuum cleaner, buckets, mops, duster, cleaning supplies and bonding insurance are among some of the items that you might need. Don't forget a signed contract and a set of keys.

Do not hire just anyone, make sure they are reliable. A fly-by-night employee may leave you when you need him the most, like when you are stripping a floor. Do a background check and a work history.

It is not good to get yourself into a lock down situation. Like a store where they lock you and your crew in for the night. One, you can't leave to check on other crews and two, if you need more equipment or supplies...your locked in.

6 – RESTROOM CLEANING SERVICE

It sounds bad but it really isn't as bad as it sounds. You find service stations, little stores, and repair shops have restrooms they don't want to clean and neither do the  employees. You charge the customer a curtain price per restroom, per time. And you pay an employee half that price but you set up a route. A restroom can be cleaned in less than 5 minutes if there is: 1stall, 1 urinal, 1 sink and is cleaned on a regular basis.

7 – COMMERCIAL RESTROOM CLEANING SERVICE

In big companies, some are going to a special cleaning service just to do the restrooms.

Multigraphic Corp. was a 900,000 sq. ft. office complex. I could not handle the $100,000 bond they wanted for clean their offices. They separated the bid and made their 25 huge restrooms which were to be cleaned 4 times a day, and only a $10,000 bond for some cleaning service to clean.

You can also sub-lease with a large janitorial service to do their restrooms so they could concentrate on the other work.

8 – STUDENT CLEANING SERVICE

I knew this guy (let's call him Ralph) who put  himself through college by hiring students at the colleges over the phone (never meeting the students) to do odd jobs for residential customers. Ralph would charge the customer, let's say the pay was $10.00 an hour with a 2 hour minimum and he would pay the student $7.50 an hour. Now the first time out, Ralph would have the customer make out the check to Ralph's Student Service and would instruct the student to pick-up the check and have it delivered to him or put in his P.O. Box. When Ralph received the check he would assigned that same student another cleaning assignment. This way Ralph always got his money first. If Ralph made $40.00 that meant the student worked 4 hours and earned $30.00 of what Ralph had. The student would work the next 12 hours (12 hours X $2.50 ((Ralph's pay)) =$30.00) receiving the money from the customer before Ralph would get another check made out to Ralph's Student Service. It is a great business but it does have a few wrinkles. #1- The customer could have the student doing jobs that a professional should do like painting or laying carpet, etc. #2- The customer would steal your student for himself and save $2.50 an hour. #3- The student if left alone could steal from the customer. #4- This all took place in the 1970's (I know it was before your time☹, fortunately, it would not matter today but back then there were "beat-nick" (young guys with goatees) and they would show-up at to the customer's door and scare her so bad that she wouldn't let them in the house to do the work. Remember, Ralph never met his students.

9 – RESIDENTIAL HANDYMAN SERVICE

If you are good with fixing things, then this might be for you. Put magnetic business cards on residential cars. But don't just say that you know how to fix something, make sure you do. If you don't fix it right you may have to go back and try fixing it again.

bite

 It could come back to   you somewhere. You know where.

10 – COMMERCIAL HANDYMAN SERVICE

Instead of having a company call a handyman service out of the phonebook, you go to companies and offer your services and hand them a smile and a business card.  Tell them thank you & turn around and leave. Don't go into detail unless they call you back. Look, if you go into detail you will be taking up the secretary's time plus it will slow you down for getting out as many business cards as you possibly can. This is a numbers game. The more business cards you pass-out the better your chances of someone calling you.

This job requires you to have good plumbing and electrical skills. KNOW YOUR CRAFT.

The average advertising rate is 2/100. That means for every 100 business cards that you give out to companies only 2 companies will call you. This rate 2/100 is UNIVERSAL in…..every…..thing…..you…..do.

TRUST ME…..EVERYTHING

CHAPTER 4

OUTSIDE
THE BOX

BLACK TIE

When I had my janitorial business, I also had a home repair business, a commercial painting business and I took (2) two R.E. (Real Estate) classes at college to get my "property management certificate". This way I had more skills than the regular run of the mill janitorial service. It gave me the edge.

When I was giving my janitorial business away after the divorce, one of my best employees who had worked for me for about 1 ½ years, wanted to start his own janitorial business (he wanted to call it "The Mop N Pail" I tried to talk him out of that name but with no luck). One of the accounts he got was an antique shop. The shop owner told him of a "Black Tie" dinner they had recently gone to. This dinner was being held by an advertising couple in their home. They had invited about 25 guests. After a short period of time the dinner was being laid out in the dining room and the guess were asked to take their seat for dinner.

They were just about to eat when the hostess got up and said; "I am so excited, I can't wait until after dinner to show you our new project". She gets up from the table and went upstairs to find what she wanted to show everyone. Now, this was a "Black Tie" dinner (which is getting cold). She came down the stairs with this sphere in her hand and she opens it up and said; "We are going to put nylon stockings inside the sphere and call the item "Leggs". Now to you younger crowd, you wouldn't remember but us older folks recall that this was revolutionary just like the "hula-hoop". Can you imagine, an item the shape of an egg with nylons (nylon stockings were very popular back in my ancient days) inside and then calling them "Leggs"? It was an instant success. Now, that was thinking "outside the box".

CHAPTER 5

MILLION DOLLAR

PROJECT

MT. ST. HELENS

Back in 1979, Mt. St. Helens erupted, blowing a side and the top of the mountain into the

atmosphere and around the world. The mountain erupted for many days and the heavy ash was seen around the world falling out of the sky to the ground every day for at least a month. I had another janitorial service this time in Portland, Oregon. I went to Yakama, Washington (that was 90 miles from Mt. St. Helens, it was too dangerous to get closer) and got some ash for myself. The ash was adrift about 20 feet high next to the buildings. I put 700 pounds of the ash into heavy duty garbage bags. I don't know why, I was stupid. I brought it home and proceeded to put an ounce of ash into little baggies to sell it for a $1.00 an ounce. I wore a surgical mask but only worked for 15 minutes at a time and had to stop for 30 minutes. The ash was so dense that if you took your hand and pushed it against a wall as HARD AS YOU CAN that was the feeling I felt on my chest after 15 minutes working with the ash. I said to myself; "Self, this is

a real good way to kill yourself but not a good way to make money". I tried different things,

 but the density of the ash would

not hold together. And then I got a "brilliant" idea (I told you that I was stupid). I had a closet in the middle of my basement, why it was there I don't know to this day. Anyway, I made the closet into a vertical furnace. Insulating it on all 4 sides and I put a small heater on the floor of the closet. I then made 15 racks to hold 4 throwaway cupcake tins per rack and I shaped each cupcake to the shape of Mt. St. Helens the way it erupted taking out the side of the mountain. I then put Pam cooking spray in the cupcake tins so they wouldn't stick and filled them with cement.

In 1 ½ hours the little volcanoes were done. I took my little Wagner spray paint gun and with 10% Elmer's Glue/ 90% water, I sprayed the little mountains with the glue. I had 2 giant ceramic salt and pepper shakers and I filled them with the ash to sprinkle over the glued mountains. I cut off a piece of tailpipe and sharpen one end. I bought some felt and folded it, I think, 8 times. Then I took the tailpipe and a sledge hammer and pounded the tailpipe over the felt and made 8 perfect circles which I used to place on the bottom of the pre-glued little mountains.

I was sitting on my couch with 2 perfect replicas of Mt. St. Helens on my coffee table along with my "happy as a peacock" feet when the doorbell rang. It was my Electrolux vacuum cleaner salesman. He was a young college student who never got his hands dirty. He was at my door to pick-up 3 of my vacuum machines for repairs (remember, I still had a janitorial business). We talked for bit about my volcanoes replicas and about Mt. St. Helens always being in the news. I said; "Wouldn't this be neat (that is the way we talked back then) as the <u>Pet Volcano?</u> Put the replica in a box with some Easter grass and a card that says to visit your mother every 100 years". What an idea it was. You see, just about 5 years earlier a guy came up with "The Pet Rock", it sounded stupid at the time but he made millions from the idea. Anyway, my vacuum cleaner salesman thought it was really a great idea. He said that he knew of some people that had money and might be willing to sponsor me. I let him take one of the little volcanoes (first mistake). Three days later he came back from Salem, Oregon, the capital of the state, where he had the volcano trademarked "The Pet Volcano". He had stolen my idea. He said that he would go across the country, getting orders for the Pet Volcanoes and that he would pay for all my supplies (he never saw my work station in the basement, good idea), of cement, glue, felt etc. and give me $.35 for each volcano sold. I asked him how he was going to go all over the country. Have you ever seen one of those wallets that when you open it up an accordion of pictures would fall out? Well he had one but instead of pictures, he had credit cards.

He thought that his first stop would be in Salt Lake City where the guy lived who created the Pet Rock. And then off to Chicago. I said; "If you go the Chicago, stop in at one of the 11 Marshall Field's Department Stores (it is like Macy's in New York), they have a special section for one of a kind items". He left and came back 2 weeks later with a signed contract from Marshall Field's for 50,000 volcanoes. That was $17,500.00 for me. I said; "Why did you stop? Why didn't you go on to Macy's in New York City"? He said; "They wanted 15,000 by Halloween, 15,000 before Thanksgiving and the rest of 20,000 a week before Christmas". I said; "No problem, I found an empty ceramic store and I could poop out 15,000 volcanoes a day even with the box, grass and card". He said; "I charged Marshall Field's $5.00 each and it will cost only $2.00 each. The problem is they have a clause in the contract that states if we can't make all of our delivery dates, no money would be given out. At $2.00 a box that comes to $100,000 at my end and I don't have it". I was stupid and he was stupid because sometime

 later when it was too late, I found out, we could have taken the contract to any bank and they would have loan us all the money we needed to get the job done. Good Bye millions --- Fly Away …. ☹

CHAPTER 3

100 BUSINESSES YOU CAN START WITH LITTLE OR NO MONEY

11 – SMALL SHOP WINDOW CLEANING

I had a friend that was washing windows for a living and he made about $150 a day and that was about 40 years  ago. He would literally go to the little shop and ask the owner if he would like his windows cleaned. Sometimes he would do the inside and outside or just the outside. He could estimate the job before he walked into the shop. I think, back then, he was charging $5.00 for an 8 x 10 pane one side. So you see if they had 5 panes inside and out that was $50 in his pocket. It took him about 10 minutes to do each pane. Now before you get up and go knocking on little shops in the neighborhood understand he had a knack for what he was doing. He had a bucket on wheels, his detergent, and a lamb's wool applicator to apply the detergent. He also had a pole to reach the high places, some non-streaking window cleaner, a squeegee, some paper towels, and a few rags. A janitorial retail supply store is the place to go to get the right supplies needs. My friend knew what he was doing and you should too. Test you equipment out first. Make sure your detergent does the job. And especially make sure that your window cleaner does not streak at all in sunlight otherwise you will be cleaning that window for ever. He also had a way of squeezing the whole window in one stroke. Practice makes perfect.

12 – SMALL SHOP STRIPPING & WAXING

When I had a small janitorial service I was hungry for more work, that's when I met my friend with the small shop window cleaning service. I wanted to strip and wax floors in small shops but I couldn't tell how big the floor was or how bad the owner needed my services without going inside the shop. Do you know how embarrassing it was to walk in a shop only to find that the floors were beautiful and didn't need my services and then the owner would come up to me and ask me;

How may I help you?

The window washing service guy was my ticket inside the little shop. He would work one side of the street and I would work the other side. When my friend would go inside the shop and give the owner an estimate on the windows he would look at the floors to see if they needed cleaning and talk to the owner saying; "I know of a friend who is in the janitorial business that can clean your floors for you." Myself, I would estimate for a window washing job then go inside. And while I was talking about his windows, I would be looking at his floors and coming up with an estimate the owner didn't know what hit him. It was great. Of course, my friend got more business than I did but when I got some business it was for more money.

Stripping and waxing little shop floors is a fine business but just remember that this is the type of job that you will be lock in until you are done so have all of your equipment, supplies and employees needed for the job with you. Oh! And if the owner has an alarm system he needs to let everyone know that you are cleaning the place.

I had a scary experience once when I was doing one of these shops. Fifteen minutes into the job (it was dark outside); I could see about 4 or 5 cops with guns drawn crouching under the window pane outside thinking I didn't see them. I quickly threw my hands up in the air and went to the door. Let me tell you, it is not something you want to experience, <u>EVER</u>.

13 – HOUSE PRESSURE WASHING

One of the good things about this business is  that you don't have to advertise to get the work. All you have to do is drive around and spot a house that needs cleaning. The bad thing about this business is that someone may see you driving slowly through their neighborhood and think you are stocking the area. The equipment and supplies you will need is a pressure washer which you could rent for the first few jobs, a good detergent, bleach, and a long <u>good</u> hose that doesn't kink up when you use it. I wouldn't charge more than $40 based on an hour worth of work. I say $40 because the owners can rent a machine for about that price. You will need magnetic business cards to give the customers while he thinks on you getting wet rather than him doing the work himself. There will be times when you will find a house renter instead of an owner. If that happens, try to talk the renter into keeping his place clean for the owner. Of course, if that doesn't work, try to get the owners phone number. If all fails, you can go online and look up the owner of the place which is public record with the city. By the way, the renter may say that he was planning to do it in the near future, that is a

. If he was thinking about pressure washing the house, he would have done it already. If the place is empty find the R.E. Company that is handling the house and ask them for the business. Oh! And pick a sunny day to do the work so, if you do or should I say when you get wet, it will feel good. Lol

14 – MIDDLE MAN – BUYING/SELLING

Being the middle man with any product can be very profitable. There is no overhead because you don't buy the product and store it somewhere. What takes place is that you find a product and sell it to someone else at a higher price. You need to tell the customer that this is a limited time offer so they need to act quickly. If people must act quickly, that give then no time to think or to go to Wal-Mart and compare prices.

Quickly * Today * Now Don't Wait

These are terms you need to use if you are selling anything. GLUE them into your brain.

I found an imitation mink blanket. It was about 50" x 80" the kind that you put over your body on those cold winter nights. It was selling for $12.95 at this special store. Wal-Mart had some blankets about the same size and nearly the same style except no imitation mink but they were all for $12.95 as well. Understand if customers aren't looking at the time for a blanket then they may not do any compared shopping on your item especially if your prices are low enough. I liked $29.95 because the price was low, it looked like mink, and the Eastern seaboard was facing below freezing temperatures. It made for quick sales.

15 – MIDDLEMAN – WAREHOUSELESS

This concept is similar to #14 except these products are for long term selling. What I mean is there isn't the quick sell hype like in #14. It is good to have a website although you can use Craigslist for one item or two. But for the most part, you will need a website to show off with pictures all 20 to 100 or more products. What you do is you find products that are around your area. Maybe from a mom and pop shop that is dragging their feet on expansion or sales. They are getting by with what they have and are not going big.

That is how Ray Crock put McDonald's on the map. The McDonald brothers were happy just selling their burgers in Des Plaines, Illinois.

In Newport Beach, California, a company had a great concept for building <u>above</u> ground swimming pools and putting them <u>below</u> ground at a fraction of the cost of an in ground pool. Their idea was so good that Better Homes & Garden picked them up and did a big spread of the concept and the business. In the spread the company showed off their "connecting" decks which were 2 foot deck squares that could be connected like puzzle pieces.

The company had no desire to expand any farther (to my knowledge) than the magazine spread. A person could take <u>their designs</u> (not changing the designs in any way) and boost the price of the concepts and advertise in New

York. The customer would buy from you the designs and you would buy the designs from the company and mail them to the customer at a profit. A lot of businesses are selling products on the net. It is one of the biggest businesses around and there seems to be plenty of room for one more warehouse middle man. Just try to have quality products at fairly low prices.

You need a way to collect your money. The cheapest way is a check or money order. All you need is a post office **address** not P.O. Box #. You could also take in credit card numbers. Just find a company that will allow you to take in the credit card number and you just call the number into the service to get an approval. There is also Pay Pal that will charge you with a minor fee. Whatever you decide, do not give the customer your street address if you are running your business out of your home.

PERIOD

16 – NEWSLETTER SUBSCRIBERS

Newsletters are easy and there is <u>no cost</u> to you. Just find a subject that you like and want to pass it on to you subscribers. Charge the subscribers a monthly price. Come up with articles from the

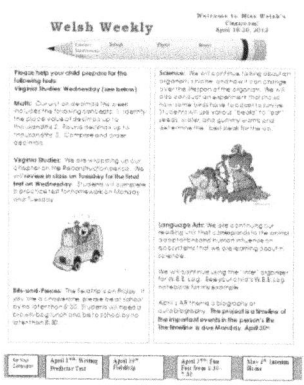

subject and type it into your weekly newsletter. E-mail them to your subscribers and you have a business. You can use Craigslist to get your subscribers. Make your

Newsletter interesting and you shouldn't have any problem getting subscribers or hanging on to them.

17 – NEWSLETTER ADVERTISIER

This business basically goes with #16 Newsletter Subscribers but there is a way to do this business without having a newsletter. What you need to do is FIND newsletters and offer to get advertisers for them at no cost. You simply charge the advertisers 10% over cost of putting the ad in the newsletter. After doing a good job for the person with the newsletter, maybe he will place an ad of yours in his newsletter for nothing. Wouldn't that be nice! This is just another business that you can do at no cost to you.

18 - FLIER ADVERTISER

This is another business that carries a "no cost to you" label in it. However it is not a wonderful job to take on as a single mission in life. It is a business that you will find goes well with another business and you just want to advertise and you don't have the money to spend at the moment.

I did this business for that very reason. First I found a small printing company. When I say small, I mean someone who was printing fliers in his garage. I made a deal for about 10 different fliers printed on both sides with a quantity of 5000. Now starts the search for advertisers who are willing to put out money for 5000 flies hand delivered in the neighborhood. Pizza places are always good for fliers but they usually don't want other pizza places going in their hand delivery run. It fairly easy to find shops that will reach into their wallets for a 5000 flier run but you need to keep your prices down. This is why you need to strike a deal with the printer. I found a printer that was willing to print 5000 on both sides for $75 including the paper. What I charged the customer was $50 for one side. So my profit for all 20 customers was $250 minus my fliers which was $37.50 (one side of $75) equaling out to $212.50 net. Now came the fun part of collating the 10 fliers which you might have the printer do it for you. Then it is just rolling them up and putting a rubber band on each of them. For every good side there is also a bad side and that would be the delivery of the 5000 fliers. Once you get into the delivery process you can understand why it is good to have 20 customers. The fliers are difficult to throw because of their weight being so light. Have fun.

19 – SIGN ADVERTISER

When I first started my tax business, I found a corrugated sign company that would print an 18 x 24 sign

TAXES

$40

PHONE# at a

dollar a piece. So I thought, as I always do, to find another person to advertise with me on the sign. Each of us would get 18 x 12 of the sign and split the cost. Now you can go one step farther and just find advertisers to place ads on a corrugated sign for a $1.50 as long as they buy 100 or more signs at a time. This way you can make $50 for every order of 100 signs to the sign company. Again, <u>NO COST TO YOU TO START UP THIS BUSINESS.</u>

20 – RENT OUT YOUR TRUCK

Renting out your truck can offset the gas and put cash in your pocket as well. People are always looking for some way to move an item from point A to point B. It is said, that if you own a truck you will never be without friends. Some furniture stores don't have delivery service. Either you can work out a delivery for a store and/or have a service where people call you to drive your truck to the store to pick-up the item (no lifting, just driving).

With this type of service

You will be charging for gas, miles, and time. Something like this: Service call to the store $20 and $5 a mile to the destination. Any waiting time over 30 minutes is another $20. Cash up front of course.

CHAPTER 6

ADVERTISING

KNOWLEDGE &

OWNERSHIP

There are three things you need to know to make your business get off the ground. They are: Bookkeeping, Taxes, and Advertising. Without these essentials, your business <u>will fail.</u> All 3 are fairly easy to learn but <u>you</u> need to understand them. Some company you hired to do the advertising, bookkeeping, and taxes for you, that company is not putting the food on your table.

I lived in Reno, Nevada way back when (1975).

The only jobs were at the casinos. A change person was an entry level position. You carried around a 40# change belt. This was way before the credit card slot machines. Anyway, I wanted to improve my situation and get rid of the belt. A friend of mine told me about this school that was just starting up. In this school, the owner was teaching 21 dealing, craps, and bartending. Each class was $300 and you were guaranteed a job upon completion of the class. So I gave him the money to take the bartending class. He was a great teacher and in a few short weeks I had learned 140 different drinks and how to "free pour". The owner was an ex pit boss and he had no problem finding me a job in a casino were I was able to make over $100 in tips every night. I WAS KNOWN FOR MY FROZEN MARGARITA.

This guy, the owner of the school, was great at teaching but in 3 short months he was out of business. He thought that word of mouth would be all the advertising he would need. It wasn't. *"HOW CAN YOU WIN THE WORLD IF NOBODY KNOWS YOU'RE THERE?"* Just because you know how to fix TV's that isn't enough if the public doesn't know you fix TV's.

Advertising is, "fairly easy" but it is not that simple. You don't just place an ad in the local newspaper. What is a newspaper? Hummm! An ad in a phone book is costly. What is a phone book? Hummm! How about placing an ad on Craigslist? Ahhh! But wait! First you need to know your audience that you are trying to reach with your business. If all you are doing is cutting lawns, maybe your best bet is to knock on doors that haven't seen a lawn mower in a few weeks.

Try to have the largest audience you can have when picking out a business card. But if your business only caters to women then you should focus on an ad that only women will see. Maybe, a fashion magazine might be the ticket.

When I started my tax business, I placed signs on telephones poles or in the ground, that read;

TAXES

$15

(904) 555-3777

It was simple to read (when cars were going 40 mph) black ink on white board. It gave the price (people want to know the price). And it was a cheap way to advertise (when you are starting out, cheap is best if it gets good results).

If you want to use color, test it out first. Get some colored paper and use different colored markers on them. You'll be surprised when you make the comparison.

Be creative. Advertise on someone else's dime if you can. When I started my house painting business, I put out flyers. But what I did was I found other businesses that wanted to use flyers (pizza businesses are great for this). The other advertising businesses paid for my advertisement and I delivered the flyers.

My tax signs were on 18" X 24" board. I had the advertising company print 2-up on each board and cut them in half. So each of my tax boards were 18" X 12". That cut my cost in half as well. Be Creative!

CHAPTER 7

HELPFUL HINTS

LOOK AROUND

YOU

WAL~MART

Wal~Mart is a perfect example of how to start a business but not how to run a business.

When Wal~Mart was getting started across America, K-Mart was "the store" and was very healthy. Wal~Mart knew if they wanted break into the market place they would have to change the way people thought about department stores.

They started with wider isles with eye catching stock in the middle of the isle. They had tons of more stock to choose from and lowered their prices to about 2 to 5 cents less than their competitors. With more check-out counters, and the store hours 24/7 this was the edge they were looking for.

But they didn't stop there. They looked to see how they could improve their employees.

Making them one happy family, they started
pep rallies and singing w...a...l squiggly (~)
m...a...r...t. every morning. The employees
were told that when they were stocking the
shelves, if a customer came up and asked
where an item was, the employees were to
stop everything and take the customer to that
item. If they didn't, they might find a "pink
slip" in with their paycheck.

Back then, they had "greeters". Their real
function was to check in return packages, so
Wal~Mart made them into "greeters" (Hi,
welcome to Wal~Mart) as well. Friendly
service was the key.

The final touch in the very beginning was to
make sure everyone knew where a Wal~Mart
store was. They did this by putting the stores
next to freeways and placing a tall enough sign
for you to see from the highway.

It wasn't until later, after they were well established, that they made most of their stores into "superstores" by adding food to their line-up. That was the straw that broke K-Mart's back.

The owner passed away some time ago and like all big companies "The Corporation" took over and their concern is to the stock holders now, not the customer.

But their example of how a new business should think before opening their doors is a model to follow **every day** because sooner or later there will be another company with greater and hungrier ideas that can put you out to pasture in a heart-beat. You're **never** too big.

CHAPTER 3

100

BUSINESSES

YOU CAN START

WITH LITTLE OR

NO MONEY

21 – HAVE TRUCK WILL TRAVEL

T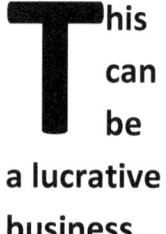his can be a lucrative business.

Just like the pick-up truck, having a real truck for hire can be a busy business if you plan it right. People want to move from where they live to somewhere else but they don't have a driver's license. Again, you are only driving your truck and not lifting a twig. Another way to utilize your truck is by going on the internet and finding a middle man services that hookup trucks with loads. One thing to watch out for is any dead head miles. Those are miles that you must travel empty. You can start this business on Craigslist. And if you don't have a truck you can rent one until you can buy one. Craigslist is a good source for buying a truck reasonable. What did we ever do before Craigslist? I think we were living in the Stone Age.

22 – TIME SHARE

I never gave Time Share a thought when I was younger but recently I met this gentleman who had bought enough time shares and now he is a gold card member and is allowed to reserve a room anywhere/anytime as long as it is available at that time slot. He can reserve it for next week or 4 months from now. These rooms are for a family to stay in with plenty of room to spare.

You can make this into a business if you plan it right. Say the Superbowl is planned for New Jersey in 2013. You can plan to fill a family room (4-8 people) as soon as you know where the Superbowl is going to be held. Maybe you charge each person $500 a piece for a week stay. With 8 people that equals to $4000 and you don't have to change the sheets plus you don't have to be there when they arrive. A once a month payment to the time share company is $250 to $400 all depending on what agreement you made with the time share company.

Another great place for a time share is Lake Tahoe or any ski resort in the beginning of winter. The tens of thousands of skiers need a place to stay and I'm sure $1,000 or more for a week is not too much.

A Craigslist ad from anywhere in the US or other countries is a good market to try out your time share business. Let the good times roll. ☺

23 – CURB PAINTING

I don't know why I am putting this business out there other than the fact it makes money. I knew a guy that did this for a living. The operative word was "living". He made a good business out of it. I just didn't like the way he had to set-up his advertising. In curb painting you paint about 6 feet of black curb and then you painted the house numbers on the dried black paint. That part was very good. I mean, how many times have you ever tried to read a house number and had to stop and look at the house closely to find the number.

The way he wrote up the advertisement and gave it to the home owners was a little sly but legal. His letterhead looked official, like it came from the department of transportation of the city. But of course, it wasn't a legal letterhead. In the letter, he made it sound mandatory that everyone would need to get their curb painted on a certain date and a payment of $15 was due into his office a week before the paint job. "AND THAT'S ALL I GOT TO SAY ABOUT THAT."

24 –FANCY DRIVEWAY PAINTING

Have you ever seen scroll work done on driveways or a sparkling covered driveway this is what I am talking about. Sherman N Williams use to have fancy driveway painting kits but even if they don't carry them anymore, I am sure you can Google it. The great thing is you can make a ton on money doing the work. And if you do a great job the customer will be happy to refer you with a ton of referrals.

The main thing is getting that first customer and maybe you give him a 20% discount. But don't tell him he is getting a discount. You just want to lower the price to get the first account. NEVER SAY *** IF YOU WILL GET US REFERRALS WE WILL GIVE YOU A DISCOUNT PRICE.

They never will

What they will do is take the discount price and you will never hear from them again. Just offer a lower price. They don't have to know that you are just trying to get your foot in the door.

25 – CHRISTMAS LIGHTS

This is a great job but it is seasonal. Did I mention that it is seasonal? OK then! The great part of the job is when you turn on the lights. Of course, the hard part is putting up the lights. After all, why do you think they hired you? PRICE ACCORDINGLY. It would probably be good to have designing skills. I would advertise with magnetic business cards and put them on cars.

26 – DOG WALKING

If you want to lose weight and you're not concerned with becoming rich, this maybe the job for you. Oh yah! It is good to like dogs too.

Like humans, dogs need to exercise too. You should walk your dog twice a day. I have 2 medium size dogs. Bonnie is 12 years old and lags behind a little when I take her out. Now Sandy is 5 years old and she just wants to go. I came up with a solution. When it gets dark I let my non-aggressive dogs out and when I get up in the morning about 4 AM I let them out again. As for myself, I walk alone and talk to my neighbors along the way.

Like I said, in this business you need to like/love dogs. People who work don't have the time to walk their dog as much as they would like. This is where you come in. Find someone who has a dog and strike up a conversation, pet the dog if you can and ask if the owner would like you to walk the dog. What is a fair price? I don't know, probably about $50 a month in nice weather (no rain or 50 mph winds) and $100 for 2 or 3 dogs. Aggressive dogs you decide. You may be able to take on another client if the dogs get along together. Good Luck!

27 – KENNEL CARE

Demanding service; owners of the pet need it from time to time, the cat or dog doesn't want it anytime, and you need

to have patients and love to do it every time. But because it is a demanding business you can get a good price for your services. Kind of like daycare service, some charge half of your weekly paycheck.

What you need is a building with a lot of cages or a lot of cages in your BIG backyard. I would check with your local city ordinances to make sure you are within the law. Advertising is a little difficult. Probably the best way is to place an ad in a weekly postal magazine. Make sure you put your business name, address (maybe a map), and of course, your phone number in the advertisement. It goes without saying that you need to know a few things about the pet, its name, shots, allergies, and any other problems the animal might have that you would need to deal with for adequate service to the pet. You should consider a form that the owners can fill out so you have it on record. The form should have the needs of the pet and also a responsible clause to protect your tail.

28 – BARNACLE BOAT CLEANING

I had a friend who was crazy enough to scrap off barnacles for a living so I thought maybe there was someone else who would be crazy to do the same thing. Lol

This is **NOT** an easy job. <u>THIS IS HARD WORK</u>. The barnacles get on the boat like leaches. They need to be removed off the boat the sooner the better. These shell fish create drag on the performance of the owner boat and the longer that they are there the harder they will be to remove (they become like cemented rocks). Price has to be determined by the hardness of the job. Boat service shops can give you an idea as to what equipment and supplies you will need. To advertise, all you need are business cards and boat owners that you can give the cards to as you carry on a conversation with him starting out with "how beautiful his boat is or could be if the barnacles were removed".

29 - WASHING N WAXING CARS – HOME

I had a friend. Why do I call everyone I meet, my friend? Actually, I never really want to see him again. We had an opportunity to rent an office that I couldn't afford by myself. I needed it for my tax business and he wanted the office for detailing. The location of the office was zoned for office business actives and not for detailing cars. Always check with the city to make sure you can perform the job you want at the working location you have picked. Advertising for detailing cars at home you might want to put signs out on the street like you would for a garage sale. Otherwise if you do an excellent job and the price is right you may find that word-of-month will be your reward. And remember,

> **In God we Trust**
> **all others pay   CASH**

30 – WASHING N WAXING CARS – BUSINESS

Believe it or not, this business can be as big as you want it to be. You can start with small businesses with a faucet for your hose and work

it to where you have a trailer with a water vat. You can hire employees that drive from company to company cleaning and waxing cars and all you do is collect the money. Remember the customers have to work all day maybe overtime. One thing they do not want to do when they get home is the cleaning and waxing of their car but they sure would like to have it done if the price is right and especially if the job the customer receives is high quality. That customer will come back to you as often as he gets his lawn done. And you can take that to the bank. To advertise your business, all you will ever need is a nice flyer or brochure (with the price on it) to give to the receptionist and a few business cards at the receptionist's desk for office people to pick-up. And you're on your way to a ton of money.

CHAPTER 8

WHAT A FLOP

When I had my Commercial Janitorial Service, a large company called Union Pacific wanting me to bid on their 10 buildings. I got the job but less than a week, and I came to realize that this place was awful to clean. The engineers and firemen would get off of work and go into the huge shower stall restrooms with their greasy hands and make a mess everywhere. Fortunately, in the commercial janitorial business you can sell a business for 3 to 6 months of the contract price. And that is exactly what I did ASAP.

CHAPTER 9

BOOKKEEPING

DO IT

YOURSELF

When I first started my janitorial business I had no idea how to do bookkeeping or what to do with my taxes. I just knew how to clean

offices. So I hired this bookkeeper to take care of my paperwork. I got into so much trouble with the IRS that it took me six years to recover. I said to myself; "SELF", you need to do your own bookkeeping and taxes. And that is exactly what I did and I am recommending that to you. **TRUST NO ONE** You are the one responsible at the end. Learn to do it yourself. I picked up the simple version of the software Quicken Books and I was on my way to good bookkeeping.

The Quicken books, simplified version is on all you need. Don't buy the deluxe version its too expensive and complicated. Plus you get a lot of bells and whistles that you don't need and probably will never use. It's in the simplified version you are shown how to plug-in the numbers and you press the button and there you are with all your profits and expenses calculated out in a "profit and loss statement" and that is all you need for your taxes. The deluxe version is good for making a prospectus for a loan.

Like I said, do your own bookkeeping. Once you get the hang of it will be so glad you did.

CHAPTER 3

100 BUSINESSES YOU CAN START WITH LITTLE OR NO MONEY

31 – SCRAPPING

This business isn't for everyone. You need to be physically strong. The good news is you don't have to punch a clock and no one is going to tell you what to do. You are your own boss. However, you will need a pick-up truck. A truck that is old enough to take the dings you're going to get but one that is a good running vehicle.

A few things you will need to know. First thing is where the scrap yards are located and how much per pound can you make for tin, steel etc. Another bit of information you will need is, what days the garbage is being picked up for each neighborhood you are planning to travel.

2 little tips: Try to get to the trash pickup site about 2 to 3 hours earlier to beat the competition. And you may want to consider doing a garage sale on the side because there will be a lot of items thrown away that are still in good condition that can be sold.

One time my neighbor threw out a refrigerator because he got a new one. That refrigerator is still working great after ten years.

Like I said before, scrapping isn't for everyone. I have a friend who does love it though and the cash isn't that bad.

32 - STARTING UP A REFERRAL SERVICE FOR GOOD COMPANIES

Advertising for customers is a key concern. I would say that the cheapest way to advertise for this business would be an advertising magazine postal mailer or maybe on placemats in restaurants or maybe Craigslist.

This advertisement is to get people to go on your website where you can sell the customer on a membership program. It is a numbers game. You need to charge a low fee for membership but you need a lot of customers to make a profit. This is one of those businesses that you will need about six months start-up money (the money needed until your membership customer numbers reach a profit level).

You'll have to do some leg-work also to find Good Companies. You will need to contact them and see if they would like to be posted on your website for free.

To make the referral companies good, you will need to do a background check or have your members do a survey on your referral companies.

33 - 34 - 35 – REFERRAL FOR DOCTORS, DENTIST, AND LAWYERS

You basically need to have a database on Doctors, Dentists and Lawyer including their hours, locations, and what they specialize in. It would also be good to have a price range on your Doctors, Dentists and Lawyers.

Advertising is the same as referrals for Good Companies #32.

You might want to combine the referral service or not. The best thing to do is check out other referral services and see what they do.

36 – 37 - 38 - REFERRAL SERVICE FOR GENERAL CONTRACTORS, PAINTERS, & AUTO MECHANICS

The information on this business can be found on # 32 Referral Service for Good Companies and # 33 Referral Service for Doctors, Dentist and Lawyers.

You might want to combine these referral services, or not. The best thing to do is check out other referral services.

When it comes to the general contractor, painters, auto mechanics, Doctors, Lawyers, or Dentists you don't have to recommend any of them unless you want to because all you are doing is giving the customer data on the service.

When it comes to these different referral services you don't have to recommend any of them (unless you want to) because all you are doing is giving the customers data on these services.

If you decide to recommend the referral services then you are taking on the responsibility that your recommendation is good and your business could hang on the balance.

Taking on several referral services could be too much work especially if they have a lot of data. Only take on what you can handle until you get more experience.

39 - GUTTER CLEANING

If I had this business, I would want to have a large wet vac with a long cord. Of course, you will also need a few ladders, a large hose, and some rags.

The nice thing is the advertisement can be done on Craigslist. You can also get magnetic business cards and canvas the neighborhood. Pricing this job is a little tricky. Basically you will price the job <u>from the ground</u>. But you can tell the customer that this is my <u>basic</u> price but if I get up their (referring to looking in the gutters) my price may change depending on the work involved. Some people might ask you how much you charge to replace the gutters? It would be good to know the price for the labor only in your head. The gutter supplies will vary a lot.

Gutters for the most part are easy to replace.

40 - TREEHOUSE BUILDING

This is truly a lost art, and yet it is fairly easy. Average carpenter skills should get you by.

More instructions and plans can be found on Google and/or go to Home Depot.

You can build a tree house up in a tree or on the ground around them. Obviously building the tree house up in the tree will cost 2 or 3 times more than on the ground.

It would be nice to have a few sketches of different tree house and a portfolio to show the customer. It also increases your price to the customer a little; they will think you are a professional.

Where, when, size, and materials are all part of your labor costs. I said materials because, if you make a bad mistake that is going to be on you.

Labor plus Supplies

That is the ticket.

Craigslist is a good form of advertise also any area that you can see kids you can find the parents and give a magnetic business card.

Don't build a tree house in the front yard

Don't build on the side of the house if at all possible either. It is a private thing and **should not** be known by cars driving by.

CHAPTER 4

OUTSIDE

THE BOX

THE IRVINE

COMPANY

This is a NOT true story but I could have been.

The city of Los Angeles, California is made up of two counties. LA County which is a business district and the home of Hollywood where the movie stars live. The other County is called Orange County which is made up of the beaches and Disneyland in Anaheim where Mickey Mouse lives ☺

Irvine, California is located at the southern end of Orange County. About seven or so miles north of Irvine is the Santa Ana Airport which is now called the John Wayne Airport. North of Santa Ana is Anaheim, California and from there 30 miles to the north is LAX. There is no one that will take you to LAX not even your mother. The traffic is so bad to get to the airport, it is bumper-to-bumper and it takes you about one hour and a half to get there. As a result a lot of business people do their traveling through John Wayne Airport.

Irvine, California was at one time, farm country. What if somebody (let's say the Irvine Co. who are the actually owns the property anyway) took the farmland and made it into four huge high-rise buildings so travelers who went through J. W. Airport could rent some office space for their company. Because the demand was so great for the use of J.W. Airport, the business companies had to sign a 99 year rental lease agreement. That way the Irvine Company could keep the buildings which gave them AAA credit plus they would never have to lease again.

This is not a true story and this is not how it happened but the Irvine Company is very real. What it does show is how a company can take farmland and build it into a multimillion dollar enterprise by just thinking outside the box.

CHAPTER 5

MILLION DOLLAR

PROJECT

DMSO

While I was hanging my head low over the "Pet Volcano" miss, a neighbor came to me about a product he heard over the news. The product was called DSMO – Dimethyl Sulforide. The person was trying to sell this "wood-by-product" for arthritis pain. I picked up a book on DMSO and after reading it, I told my neighbor, "Let's do it". We bought a few cases from the guy on the news and we were on our way. This guy was selling 100% DMSO for $5.00 an 8oz. bottle. I found out thru the book the best way to use the product was at 80%.

What was so good about DMSO, lumberjacks had been using it for the past 100 years. When they would cut down the trees, there was a lot of tree scraps and they would take these scraps and throw them into a huge vat. The sap and the tree scraps created a liquid called DMSO. When the vat was getting full, the lumberjacks would throw the tree scraps into the vat and the DMSO would splash on their arms. This made their arms feel very good. The only side effect was <u>10 seconds </u>later they could taste garlic.

We found the best way to sell DMSO was to advertise in the magazines that you found at the counter in a food store. The Enquirer at that time had 18 million readers. The only drawback was that the ½ an inch ad which cost $500.00 didn't come out for 6 weeks. We weren't sure what results we would get so we placed only the 1 ad instead of using up $3000 on an ad every week. Six weeks later, we got so many customers in the mail that we ran out of product and had to find another source. We found a pharmaceutical house that would sell us 100% DMSO at $15 a gallon. We were selling the product for $5 a 4oz bottle. Plus we were diluting DMSO by 20%. We were making about $150 profit for every gallon we bought. We went to a couple of magazines and bought 6 weeks of ads. After those results came in, my partner wanted to start up a different business. I have to mention here the business he wanted to go into was the arcade games. A lot of you don't remember that before computers, games were found at an arcade shop. Well he went in at the right time. He bought about 20 arcade machines and one of them turned out to be the biggest game ever back then called:

Packman

.

While he was taking a bath in a tub of money, I was still working on DMSO. The government was trying to stop DMSO from being sold because you could put it on your arm and it would absorb into the skin in 10 seconds. They were afraid that drug addicts would use it and with no needle marks the government would have a harder time finding the drug addicts & dealers. So I sold the product as cement cleaner. Even though it was cement cleaner; everyone knew that DMSO was being used for arthritis pain. I even had Channel 2 News in Portland, Oregon interview me about DMSO. Don't ever have an interview with the news media. I told them the benefits of DMSO and they put a spin on it their own way to sell it to their listeners. I had people *"bedridden"* with arthritis coming in my office to buy more.

The government couldn't stop me from selling DMSO so they told the pharmaceutical houses to only sell 2 gallons to a customer. So I had all my friends buying me 2 gallons of DMSO at that time, I had down-line distributors who were buying from me, several cases at a time.

I have to say right here

Because this was and <u>still is</u> a million dollar project I need to tell you the STREET SMART TRUTH about DMSO and the governments (1979) involvement. I told you that I read the book on DMSO back then. And what I found was that the EPA had conducted 150 tests and could not find any evidence that the product was bad for you. Instead, they found that the only side effect was the taste of garlic after just 10 second of applying the product on your skin. To this day 35 years later, chemist researching DMSO with almost a million findings have not found any evidence that this product is harmful. As a matter of fact, they feel with more research, that this product could be the catapult for finding a cure for skin cancer.

Back in 1979 the government (EPA) told the public the product was harmful because 1 person in Ireland who was taking several drugs at the time including DMSO had died. After investigating the incident farther they could not be certain that DMSO contributed to the death. The EPA conducted tests on animals by giving them an overdose of DMSO and concluded that the product was harmful to the public. Actually, it was the thought that drug addicts could and would get a hold of this product (which I can understand). If the public found out about the properties of DMSO it would open up a new can of worms for the DEA. Now the product is sold in health food stores across America.

Back to the business

One of my down line distributors, who never read anything about DMSO, knew of a place in Corpus Christie, Texas that we could buy DMSO. It was a petroleum company. In the book it said that DMSO is also a petroleum by-product as well as a wood by-product and with a gigantic number of orders to fill and no product to fill them, I decided to take my last $300 and go along with my down line distributor to Texas (that was my first mistake). When we arrived in Texas the down line distributor handled all transactions (this was my second mistake). We bought 15 five gallon drums of what we thought was DMSO. On the way back I got a little suspicious. It was New Year Day (yes, I missed New Year Eve) and the temperature was less than 50 degrees. I knew that DMSO freezes at 50 degrees and the drum were still in liquid form but it was a petroleum product, so I was not sure. It also smelled like petroleum. When I got to Portland, Oregon I looked at the shipping order and found that the product was not Dimethyl Sulforide but something different. I call down to the petroleum company in Corpus Christie and they told me that the product was not DMSO and that they didn't even sell DMSO. If we wanted our money back we would have to go back down to Texas and show them our shipping order (no internet back then). Goodbye million dollars. ☹

CHAPTER 3

100 BUSINESSES YOU CAN START WITH LITTLE OR NO MONEY

41 - LANDSCAPING SERVICE

Landscaping is much more than cutting lawns although you can go around and find lawns to cut and be done with it. Look, a Landscaping Service takes on a whole new meaning. It is not only cutting and trimming lawns but also planting trees and shrubs as well as trimming them. You also might be asked to water and/or pull weeds. Laying down mulch, inlay stones, and using pesticides are all part of your job description as well. It would also be good if you had some skills drawing especially if the customer wants you to design something. Everything you do is money in your pocket and if you are good they will recommend you to a friend. There are different ways to advertise but I would just use Craigslist.

42 – DELIVERYMAN FOR A SNACK SHOP

There are a lot of small snack shops and small restaurants that can't afford to hire employees to deliver their sandwiches and such. All you need to do is go up to these small shack shops and say that you will be glad to deliver their

snacks for a $1 per customer of which the owner can tack a delivery cost of $1 so that the snack shop doesn't have to pay a dime. I know you're saying that you can't make any money at a $1 per customer. You are forgetting the tips from the customer. One snack shop may not be enough for the lifestyle you want. So just get another snack shop in area of a different kind of menu and you will be all set.

43 – DELIVERYMAN FOR SMALL BUSINESS SHOPS

When you are buying a house there are a lot of paperwork that has to go from banks to mortgage lenders to courthouses and back to the banks again.

I worked for a delivery service that did just that. In six months' time they were a million dollar company with about 145 drivers.

There are a lot of businesses that need a delivery person where they don't ask for a huge security bond. A tax company may want you to deliver papers to the IRS. A general contracting business might need a set of plans at the courthouse. A construction company may want you to pick up some supplies. An auto parts place may have you pick up some parts at a parts warehouse or have some part delivered. The deliveries are endless and it is much cheaper for you to get the supplies if the price is right, then for a company to send an employee. Businesses are all about time and money.

44 - SHARPING KNIVES

A very lost art! A long time ago before my time, people used to come by the neighborhood with their carts and yell out "knives sharpening". Now you would find it best to put a magnetic business card on each residential car you see.

You will have to bring your portable knife sharpening equipment to the customer when they call. Everyone is in need of having their knives sharpened from time to time and if you keep your prices reasonable you should do quite well.

45 – ROOFERS

You can't pay me enough money to be a roofer. There is not enough money in the world. But that doesn't mean that one of you crazy people out there wouldn't mind going into the business. After all, someone has to do it and it might as well be you. Lol

This job isn't easy nor is it fun. Those that do this line of work, do it for the money. And there is a lot of money in this business.

Roofing, for the most part is done towards the summer when there isn't that much rain. And there is the rub, when it is 80 degrees outside;

it is 100 degrees on the roof. And if that wasn't bad enough, a pack of roofing tiles is at least 40 #s. Did I mention about the slope of the roof or the hot tar used to seal the seams?

You should never be without work. Homeowners are always finding leaks and they have to hire someone to do the work. Homeowner's insurance usually pays for the job.

Finding the leak can be a huge problem. You need to have the experience and have earned your salt or you may never find the source of the leak, unless you are extremely lucky. The best way is to work for a roofing company for about a year to get the experience you need to make a good judgment call as to the source of the leak. Because in this business you are between a rock and hard place, if you say that you know where the leak is. Then, you are responsible for the job. If you say you don't know where the source of the leak is then you don't have the job. The homeowners are going to want you to fix JUST the leak and they are going to want a guarantee, otherwise it may cost them $10,000 to $20,000 or more to take care of the problem. And if the leak comes back, guess who will be fixing the leak for nothing.

A whole lot of money, no advertising expense on Craigslist, and just a few tools to buy. These are the only good parts about this business. Good Luck!

46 – GENERAL CONTRACTOR

General contractors are the ones who orchestrate all the work on a construction site. He is the boss and gets the carpenters, plumbers, electricians, painters, and the handymen to work together to get the job done on time and in budget.

In my area, anyone can get a General Contractor's license. It is not like that everywhere in the country. The electricians and the plumbers etc. pull their own permits.

It is a great business. Your main concerns are keeping the job under budget and orchestrating the work.

Advertising on Craigslist and maybe an advertising postal mailer magazine could be helpful.

The hardest part of the job is the estimating. A general price range for supplies is OK but the labor price needs to be "spot on". If the labor price is too low you may be selling your house and your car to cover your losses.

47 – SCREEN ENCLOSURES

This job can't be done by yourself, you need a good reliable helper; otherwise you will be dangling on a ladder all by yourself with no one at the other end.

Most customers want screen enclosures for their swimming pool and/or patio so the bugs and leaves don't become a problem. You will need to know labor and materials before summiting a bid to the customer. The customer doesn't want to buy any supplies; it would be too complicated for him.

If the job is done well and at a reasonable price, he will be glad to tell his other pool friends about you but until that day arrives it might be a good idea to advertise on Craigslist and/or in a postal mailer magazine. Your ad needs to show your website because you need a website to show off your finished product and explain exactly what you can do for your potential customers.

48 – SWIMMING POOL MAINTENANCE

It is

 that

you know how a swimming pool works.

DO NOT GUESS.

This is what the job is all about. Making sure the pump is running properly is half the battle. Removing all the leaves and keeping a good PH level balanced in the water is the other half of the job.

To advertise for this job I would "Google Earth" to find which homes have pools and send them a nice letter along with a magnetic business card to put on their fridge.

The only other thing you might want to consider is t-shirts with your company name on them. The neighbors might want to know who it is going into their friend's backyard. A good idea is to register with police in that area. It will save a lot of embarrassment.

49 - 50 - 51 - PLUMBER – ELECTRICIAN – CARPENTER

I put these 3 businesses together because even though they are different in their talents they have a very common thread as to how they should run their businesses.

There was a friend of mine who lived in the ghetto and just did handyman work whenever he could find it to put food on the table. His wife left him over mounting bills but he didn't let his problems get the best of him. He saved-up some money and took an Electrician's class. A few months later when he finished school, he contacted Lowes and asked if he could install some of their electrical equipment that they have sold to their customers. House fans and AC units come to mind. His new business

E nabled him to buy a new truck and a house down in Orlando, Florida.

There are plumbing, electrician, carpenter, welder, auto mechanic, bookkeeping, tax consultant, R.E. schools. But you already knew that, right! Then what are you waiting for.

GET CERTIFIED!

And start your own business today. These professions are always in demand and the pay is GREAT. If you don't have the money right now then start saving it in your piggy. I put all my change in my piggy. And he gets fat quickly. Also the government will pay you to get schooling through Grants. I didn't say that they may pay you; I said that they will pay you. Check it out online. You will still need a piggy for your tools and equipment the profession will require of you. SO what kind of car and where are you going to buy your house when the money starts rolling in? Lol

CHAPTER 7

HELPFUL HINTS

SKILLS

What are threaded throughout this book are businesses that, for the most part, can be started with little or no money. But none of them mean "two hoots" if you don't have the skills to market them to the customers.

The Navy gave me the skills I needed to start my janitorial service. I was a "deckhand" in the Navy. My job was to make sure that the back end of our ship was clean. We had 30 deckhands for this task. I had 15 men on the starboard side (right) and someone else had 15 men on the port side (left). We hosed down and then mop the decks, sanitized the heads (big restrooms) on a daily bases. Our job also was to chip, wire brush and paint the saltwater rust from the decks. Once a week we would strip and wax the floors inside the compartments. And I did this for four years.

I'm telling you this because when I started my janitorial service and had to shake the hands of company owners, my hands were calm and dry. It carried skillful assurance to the table when we talked. The owner's hands were sweating. He was unsure of the cleaning end of his business and was hoping that I was a right man for the big job of cleaning and maintaining his building. With my confident dry hands, I knew I had the job even before I gave the owner the bid. My confidence that I showed was all he needed to assure himself that I was the right man for the job.

In every business you need the skills that it takes to convince the customers that you are the right man for the job. Don't think you know, make sure you know.

The job may look real easy but there is <u>always</u> more to the business than meets the eye.

People think the painting business is easy especially when they watch me paint because I make it look easy. It took a lot of years of experience to make it look easy. There is a saying in the professional painting circle, you can tell how much experience the painter has by the amount of paint he has on himself after a day of painting. If you ever had to paint a room then you know what I'm talking about. I paint a room and I may not have to wash my hands. You paint a room and you probably will need a bath. Lol

If you don't have the skills that it takes then, you need to get some. Actually, that is a good thing, especially if you work for a company to get the skill. You will not only walk away with the experience but now you will know how your competition does the work. And if you go back to school to get the skills, you will have some insight into the business that the competition may not have thought of.

Some skills can be found by googling it on the Internet. Whatever it takes, it will save you all the headaches, time, and money spent on the new business. It might even save the business itself.

CHAPTER 8

WHAT A FLOP

THE CONTRACT

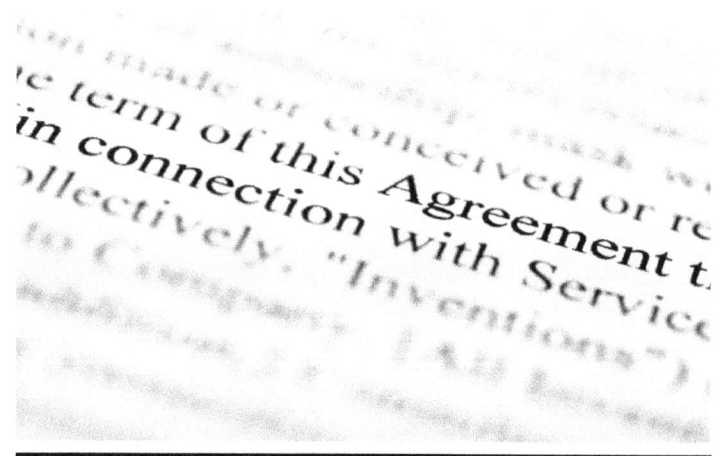

One of my first big painting jobs I ever did was without a contract. It was a big house with cheap shag carpeting. My job was to paint the inside and outside of the house, do the repairs throughout the house, shampooing the carpet, and cleaning the kitchen and bathrooms. Two of the bathrooms were in the master bedroom. The master bedroom had build-in shelves for dressers.

This job would have been fine except the owner wanted it done in three days. I had a janitorial service at the time and most of my 11 employees agreed to help me for one of the three days because it was over Labor Day weekend and they were out of school.

My wife and I worked through the night on to the second day and we had a hire from the labor pool, 5 winos for the last day (you had to watch them every minute). But the owner's wife came over and saw the college students and she came over later to see the winos. I got job done in the three days but when she came back to pay me she only paid half of what I was asking. She said she didn't like the college students (too young) but the winos she liked. I made no money and had to finish paying my students out of my own pocket. That was the last time I ever did a job with no contract. I could have taken her to court if I would have had a contract. She liked the work but she didn't like my helpers. I would have won in court. **"Never work without a contract."**

CHAPTER 3

100 BUSINESSES

YOU CAN START

WITH

LITTLE OR NO

MONEY

52 – RESIDENTIAL CARPET CLEANING SERVICE

 This is a great business but you will need to reach into your pocket a little to get it started. Good vacuums and good shampooers are a must plus professional shampooing liquid and spot removers. When I say professional liquids I don't mean what you can find in a supermarket. These products and your equipment should be bought at a janitorial outlet store. You can start out at a supermarket to buy equipment and supplies but if you want to do a professional job every

time then you'll need to go to a janitorial supply house.

When estimating a job don't just listen to the customer over the phone as to how much carpet they have to clean. You must eyeball the work.

There are too many variables. What size the carpet is (the customer may not tell you the truth over the phone)? What shape is the carpet in? It may need replacing; especially if the house pets have made messes. The flooring underneath may need cleaning and sealing to get the odor out. How thick is the carpet and are there any stairs? All stains are factors to consider as well. After all, time is money. Is there any furniture to be moved? Some furniture you can use plastic coasters under the legs (there is metal under every leg of furniture and if it gets wet it will leave a rust mark). And if the furniture is too heavy to lift by yourself who is going to help you?

53 – CARPET AND FLOOR INSTALLER

Don't leave home without a strong back, knee pads, a good back brace, and some strong guys to do all the work.

Installers lay carpet as well as, installing laminated tile squares, laying linoleum, wood tile, and ceramic tile, to name a few.

I think people should eat off the subfloor that way there would be no installing. ☺ Speaking of subfloors; when you are installing any flooring material, that subflooring should be as "sound as a dollar". And if you are at the subfloor you might want to level it first.

166

Money in this business is great but it comes with a price to pay in years after. If you are walking away from this job with no back problems then you are lying or you are one in 1000 to say that.

If you are removing carpet just be-careful that the carpet isn't glued down. A lot of commercial offices and stores are like that. Ouch!

When you are pricing this work, price the labor- only in your estimate. That is enough. There are a lot of things to consider in your bid; the size of rooms is only one factor. What if the floor needs repair or leveling? And what if the flooring has to come up and of course, what flooring is going to be put down?

The customer picks out the flooring. Don't even think about adding material prices to the estimate.

So when you submit a bid <u>don't say</u> my price is $X.00 a square foot and that includes the floor material. <u>Trust me on this one.</u>

54 – TREE TRIMMING AND REMOVAL

BIG EQUIPMENT = BIG BUCKS

You only need a few pieces if equipment that I'm sure you have lying around the house.

A utility truck bucket, back hoe, chainsaws, tree saws, tree axes, explosives, a tree mulch maker, a truck to haul the mulch in, thick chains, thick ropes, ladders, and some husky guys to handle the trees.

This can be a dangerous job. You have to keep your wits about you. Knowing which way the tree is going to fall and making sure it doesn't break a power line or crush a car. These are top priority problems.

If you are thinking you can start this business was a ladder and chainsaw, think again. That might be okay at grandma's house but it really isn't practical.

You also need to check with the city to see if you need a permit.

55 - 56 - 57 – PORCH/DECK DESIGNING, BUILDING, AND PAINTING

In Reno, Nevada is a suburb called Sun Valley and it's one of the largest or <u>the</u> largest mobile home park in the US. Mobile homes are always in the need for a nice deck with a set of stairs.

Designing a deck takes a little skill and maybe a house design software program. It would be good to have a nice portfolio of different designs for the customer to choose from.

The customer may want you to build the structure. Now you become a general contractor hiring a carpenter to build the deck and a painter to seal the deck. This whole operation may take a building permit. You need to check with the city.

Pricing a job like this might require an estimate from a carpenter and a painter before you could submit your bid to the owner.

171

If it is to be a large deck and patio you might want to consider a screen enclosure and maybe a roof as well.

Google should be a helpful tool for creating and building a nice patio/deck area.

58 – REGULAR GARAGE AND DRIVEWAY PAINTING

The business sounds easy enough and it is basically. There are just a lot of steps to go through to get a finish product.

Most garages have lots of oil on the floor. The best way to handle this problem is to pressure wash with a heavy detergent but made sure you rinse thoroughly and let the floor dry.

While we are waiting for the floor to dry, let me just say that you need to plan this job when you have about 10 nice days outside.

After the floor dries you need to check for any cracks especially in the driveway and patch them. If there are any weeds growing in the cracks you might want to use weed killer first.

Now that the cracks are sealed it is time to make the driveway beautiful. Get sealant paint. Don't use it sparingly and put down two coats, one coat is painted in one direction horizontal and other coat is painted in the other direction vertical. That way you are covering all the imperfections.

Let the sealer dry thoroughly for two days per coat. Paint may feel dry on the outside but it is still wet on the inside. Have you ever opened up an old can of paint and found a skin of paint but underneath that skin was wet paint.

Get good **not cheap** garage paint and place each of the three coats in a crisscross pattern and allow each coat to dry thoroughly.

That's it, you are finally done. Supplies and labor is in your estimate and craigslist is your advertiser.

No one should drive or park on the painted floor for at least three days after the last coat is applied.

59 – DESIGN TRIPS FOR BIG CHURCHES

This is a fun business, and is good money, and after about three years you won't have to do hardly any work for your money. Praise the Lord!

The job requires a lot of leg work that is what we used to call it before computers and cell phones. What you need to do is Google Christian places to go; retreats, cruise ships, Christian towns, and Christian sites. Contact these places and find out when they are available

God

Bless

America

plus what they have to offer and for how much for a group. Plus how big of a group is enough. Ask for brochures with all the information on them except the price. Once you get the brochures mailed to you, now you can go to the big churches with the brochures and give them your price which should be 10% higher than the actual tour.

You will need to get a non-refundable down payment to reserve the tour. And the full amount of the trip should be paid a few weeks before the actual trip.

Also you might have to rent buses and plan for meals. A singing group and a speaker can be very important as well.

There is always a "theme" behind every trip; women's retreat, seniors retreat, singles cruise, couples getaway, children's Ranch retreat etc.

Several trips are needed to be planned for each big church. That way, each church can plan a trip accordingly to their budget and schedule. And they will be needed to be planned for over a year in advance to meet the church needs. That means no pay until the planned trip goes into effect maybe six months to a year or so down the road. Plan to stay on your paper route until the money starts rolling in.

You can also have the choir or the pastor of the big church, be the guest speaker or singing group for some other big church retreat. There are all kinds of possibilities.

With a couple of years of activities under your belt the only thing you will have to do is reschedule the trips and occasionally find new retreats to go to. It is called semi-retiring, you will love it.

60 – DESIGN TRIPS FOR SMALL CHURCHES

These plans are about the same as the big churches except small churches of less than 300 Christians will find it hard or impossible to plan a trip because you need a certain amount people to make-up a group (20, 30, or 50 people). And basically most churches can only raise about 5 to 10% of their congregation to participate in a trip. So what you will need to do is get several small churches to group together. It takes some finessing but it can be done.

A lot of Christians would like to meet other Christians of the same belief. It can be a win – win situation. Good Luck!

CHAPTER 4

OUTSIDE

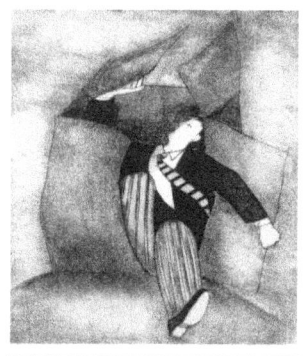

THE BOX

LAKE HAVASU

In 1964, Robert McCulloch made a deal with the state of Arizona to buy up the deserted land in the middle of nowhere that is now known as Lake Havasu for **FREE**. All he needed to do was develop the land.

Even though the land is located on the Arizona side of the Colorado River which divides California and Arizona, it was, at the time, in the middle of nowhere. The closes cities were Las Vegas to the North about 85 miles and Phoenix, Az. some 85 miles to the East. He had a hard time convincing investors to buy some of the land for developing.

It wasn't until he bought the London Bridge from England in 1967 and brought it over to Arizona, stone – by – stone, before he finally got buyers to open-up their wallets.

It took McCulloch about 4 years to build the bridge on dry land and then he dredge a canal under the bridge to create an island in the middle of the Colorado River.

 The 930 foot London Bridge is now a tourist haven for 1,000's of retired people plus sailboat enthusiast all summer long.

The city of Lake Havasu now has a population of 52,000 people plus an airport, all because of one man's vision and thinking outside the box.

CHAPTER 10

TAXES

THIS CHAPTER IS IN HERE BECAUSE YOU NEED TO DO YOUR OWN TAXES.

I know you don't like the idea because you think taxes are just too complicated. That notion is so far from the truth. Once you have learned taxes you'll be so glad you did.

You can go to H&R Block and take their basic course which cost 3 to 4 hundred dollars. Or buy "Turbo Tax" software and give it a try. Stop hiding behind your mother's skirt and get some grit. "It's easy!"

I hand write people's taxes in less than 10 minutes and most of that time is spent with their name and address. AND YOU CAN AS WELL. I go online to IRS.gov/forms and click on the 1040 form. You can type right on the form and then print it out. I will go over some basic lines in this chapter. So please, dust off your computer, go online to IRS.gov/forms and print the 1040 form. That way you can follow what I am saying.

While you are warming up your computer, let me just say, only use the 1040 form not the 1040A or the 1040 EZ. Stick with that form every year.

Let the booklet be your friend. It shows line by line what to do. (Don't print out the booklet you will use all your ink)

If you have the form in front of you then let's get started. If you are doing taxes for yourself or for someone else, breath, it's simple. LINE 7 is for all the income on a W-2 that the person made that year working for someone else. Add all the W-2s and "round-up" all the pennies ($8,963.50 = $8,964.00). LINE 8: is bank (or stock) interest. There should be a 1099 INT for that. If it is 1,500 or more, check the booklet. If you have a business than LINE 12 is your next stop. Your total profit or (-loss) from the business goes there. The total profit or loss is found on the bottom line of the Schedule C that you will need to fill out IF YOU OWN A BUSINESS. The booklet can help you on that. LINE 13 you probably won't need. It is Capital Gains. This can be a little tricky but just remember; if you bought low and sold high, the difference is Capital Gain. And the government wants to tax you on <u>all</u> your income.

Don't get me started on what they do with all our money.

LINES 15, 16, and 20 are just more income that you worked your whole life for that the government is holding out their big hands for. These are <u>IRA's</u> (saving from working for a company), <u>Retirement</u> (20 or so years working for a company), and <u>Social Security</u> (from being 62 or older). You will have to use the worksheets in the booklet if these apply to you. All the other lines on page 1 are self-explanatory and may not apply to you. Although, the last line (which should be) LINE 37 is your AGI (Adjusted Gross Income). You need to add all the other lines and put the total answer on your AGI line. This is the most important line on page 1. This is the <u>IRS reference line</u>.

Transfer the total of your AGI line to the top of page 2 (which should be LINE 38). It is all down-hill from here. ☺

LINE 39 is the <u>standard deduction</u> that the government gives you for living in America. Now, you can subtract that from your income on line 38 or you can "itemize" your living expenses but they should be more than the standard deductions or it isn't worth the effort. I would say if you don't own a house just use the standard deduction for now. Schedule A for itemize deductions are explained in the back of the booklet.

LINE 42 is a deduction that you take for each member of your household that you are supporting including yourself. Once you subtract that figure now you have the actual amount the government wants to tax you on. In the booklet are the tax tables to follow. That figure goes on LINE 44. THIS IS WHAT YOU OWE THE GOVERNMENT. Hopefully, you already have given what they wanted through your Federal Withholding Tax that is on your W-2 which is recorded on LINE 62.

EIC (earned income credit) can be added to your Federal Withholding Tax to offset what taxes the government wants. Of course this is for any children that you support and even if you don't have children. Check it out in the booklet. All the other lines are self-explanatory. And you're done.

The only other thing is your business which goes on a Schedule C and needs to be filled out before you do your 1040 form because the bottom line total will be recorded on LINE 12. The information is in the back of the booklet.

Basically, a Schedule C allows you to subtract your expenses from the profit you made throughout the year.

You send in your money if you owe or no money and just the forms to the correct address on the back page of the booklet.

If you still don't understand then it is your fear of the IRS. Read over this chapter again and read the instruction booklet page by page. If you make a mistake the IRS will correct it but see a tax consultant before agree with the IRS figures.

Listen, "bottom line", you are responsible for your own taxes no matter who does them. Don't get rid of this book because sooner or later you will be filling out your own taxes. And the sooner you learn the sooner you can be doing other people's taxes and make more money. Good Luck – You'll need it. ☺

CHAPTER 3

100 BUSINESSES YOU CAN START WITH LITTLE OR NO MONEY

61 – DESIGN TRIPS FOR COMPANIES

Extra good companies like to treat employees with a Thank You, by having trips to Las Vegas, Hawaii, or even New York (when there is a related convention in town).

Yeah, I know they can go through a travel agency but if you could provide them with a special wrinkle in the package like a guest speaker or going to the New York Giants football game (that is when the team gets out of the cellar) .

Your competition is keen and you need to think outside the box. Maybe you can combine it with other groups so the price is super low.

The incentives becomes, not only the big bucks but if you plan it right you might feel to go with the group (if you like) that is going to Hawaii.

Give the boss of the company some ideas that he can or you can work with the employees to do something wild on the trip. Maybe a scavenger hunt (don't knock it until you have tried it) with a twist at the end. Maybe you divided into groups like different departments and whoever wins is to be pampered at a beauty spa and the team that loses gets to take a mud bath.

There is also the eating contests, mud wrestling, paint ball fights, a treasure hunt or how about a Pig Out? In a pig out everyone goes to a banquet dinner and they get to pick the foods they want to eat, what they don't know is that they will not have any knives, forks or spoons. Plus each of them will have a Styrofoam cup on their nose --- thus a Pig Out.

If pictures are taken of things going wild, the trip will be one, the employees will <u>never</u> forget. And because you planned it, you are in for the planning of another trip someday, to have more fun. Everyone wins including the employees who now, will almost never leave the company and can't wait for more fun. The whole idea is to make it something that they would never do on their own. And believe me they will want to come back for more.

Did you know this becomes a huge write off for the company? If you have speakers that talk about your business or any planned activity that is business related this becomes a huge write off plus everyone has fun.

62 – DESIGN TRIPS FOR PEOPLE

Groups like senior citizens or doctors/nurses, women only, singles, and families with children are just a few groups that would love to get together for some fun like I mentioned in #61 – Trips for Companies.

Each group is different for what might be fun for them. Senior and single groups might enjoy a dance mixer, where doctors and nurses would like white-water rafting. And houseboat camping for kids and their parents is a great way to bond. If the kids are by themselves, they might enjoy a ranch with a petting zoo brought to them or maybe a turtle race. A good inspiration of different ideas that they would never forget is that TV series Amazing Race.

Information on how to start this business is found on #59 – Trips for Big Churches.

63 – SELLING WATER

Water and air are not free anymore. At gas stations that air and water pumps for a car costs $.25 to one dollar for about 10 minutes of time. And that's if you can find air and water pumps. The next thing that they are going to get rid of is all the phone booths. Oh! Yeah! They already have gotten rid of them. Poor Superman! ☹ lol

Some people are trying to live the healthy life and in the process they are drinking more bottled water than ever before. Tap water usually doesn't taste good. And if a survey was taken, you would probably find that most people would say that tap water isn't good for you.

Basically, those that are selling bottled water are just taking water from different sources and filtering it through charcoal.

Bottling the water is the hard part. Unique safety caps, bottles, and barcodes for distribution.

Competing with the stores is difficult. I'm sure that Walmart brand isn't making much profit over cost. It is their way of getting customers in the store. Finding another outlet is the ticket like vending machines or baseball games.

64 – GARAGE SALES

Garage selling is easy, just set out your unwanted stuff and sit back and wait for the money to roll in. <u>WRONG.</u>

There are many things that can be done to get maximum dollars into your pocket.

I had a neighbor that had a garage sale every week-end but she never made much money. The same items were there week after week.

Signs – People do 2 stupid things when they make their own signs. First, trying to be creative by using multicolored felt-tip pens on the signs. At 40mph, cars might be able to read about every 5th letter on the sign. The second mistake is filling-up the sign board with too many words. People are not <u>reading</u> the sign at 40mph, they are <u>glancing</u> at it.

GARAGE SALE

THAT'S ALL YOU NEED. "Lead them, and they will follow".

How can you win the world if nobody knows you're there? Just buy signs at the neighborhood store.

Now let's tackle the bigger problem. People are driving slowly but they're not stopping, they just drive away. Tell me you're not putting clothes out in front for the cars to see. **YES YOU ARE**. Put the interesting items in front and put the clothes on the side or in the back. **Everyone knows you have clothes.** Why? Because most garage sales have clothes. LOOK! If it isn't the clothes then it is the size of your yard sale.

A friend of mine of whom I have known for the past ten years goes to thrift stores <u>every week</u> sometimes <u>every day</u>. She is always on the lookout for gifts that she can give her grandchildren. Plus she rents houses and she like to "stage" them to make them more appealing when she shows them off to potential renters. The problem after all these years is; she has, in her house, a lot of little items just filling-up every corner. I suggested a garage sale and she thought it was a good idea. But after a month of sorting through everything, she could only part with about 10' X 10' space of items laid-out on the floor. I said to her that the yard needed to be filled with items to make it interesting enough for people to stop. If the people see so much stuff that they can't tell what you have then they will have to stop and get a closer look. ☺

Now that you got the customer to stop and take another "look see", you're not done yet. When you place the small items on a table, put a solid color cloth underneath to have your items "stand out". By the way, all items must be clean and in good working order. You may need an extension cord ready just in case. Don't forget to put the prices on the items. If you don't have the prices out there, the customer will not ask, they will just think that the item is too high and move on.

Now here comes the "bad" part. "They" (and I don't know who "they" are) have taken a survey across the country and have found that the best overall price is 8% of the new retail price. I don't care if you just bought the item. If you opened it, now it becomes a used item at a garage sale. If you can't part with the item at such a ridiculously low price, you might want to consider Craigslist.

While you are trying to set-up, Professional garage people will want to look at your items earlier to beat out the regular customers. That would be ok except they will be disrupting you from setting-up on time and they want your best items at a huge discount. Judge these Professionals for what they are. If you're not sure that you can sell the items they want at a much higher price then ask them for their phone # and tell them that if these items are still here after, say, 2PM, I will be willing to sell them to you at your price. See what they say. lol

65 – MASTER GARAGE SELLING

Now if you know how to do a garage sale it is time to graduate to professional or master garage selling.

Like I mentioned in my last segment at the end of #64 - garage selling, that is what pro's do. They come to a garage sale a little early and try to buy the whole lot or a portion of the lot for their own sale. That way they can make a nice profit. Time is on their side. You as a yard sale owner are looking for a fast sale, were the pro has weeks to sell the same items. Fast talking! Fast money! Fast pick-up truck! And before you know it, a portion of your garage sale lot is gone at a fraction of what it might be worth because you were afraid that your sales would be too low.

A master seller knows what a yard sale market can bare. The only goes after the "hot" ticket items. A junk table might be to his liking if the price is right. Let's say, you have a junk table of 30 items at $.10 each ($3.oo table) the pro will say I will buy it all for one dollar, knowing that he can probably sell each item for $.20 each.

If you have a scrapping business already you might want to combine a master garage selling business with it. Hey, it just might pay the rent and then some.

66 – WAREHOUSE FLEA MARKET

Now that is the ticket. Get about 5000 ft.^{2} of warehouse space (you might have to get a permit or license) section off 10' X 10'spaces and start a warehouse flea market.

The sectioned off spaces will pay for your warehouse space and electricity. That way, your area is free and with all those clients you can become a master seller.

The best thing about a warehouse flea market to the clients is; it becomes a great security and weather issue. No one can just walk in and steal from someone's table without you knowing it. And the weather is never a factor.

If you get some vending machines you can make a percentage off of them as well. Great business!

67 – INTERNET GARAGE SELLING

The heaviest item you will be working with is a camera. Find places like Big Lots and take pictures of the items you want to sell online. You will need a website to show off your items and you will need to advertise on craigslist about your website.

You can also check out other websites or items you believe would be good on your website.

When you get a customer have them send you the money plus shipping by way of PayPal or credit card, then contact the person with the item, pay him and have them send the item to your customer's address or by mail to your address. Then ship off the customer's box with your P.O. Box that has an <u>address</u> to it.

Because your items are small you make most of your money on shipping. That is why those TV ads can sell you 2 for the price of one because they make the customer pay separately for the shipping and handling. What a gimmick but it works.

68 – SELLING DMSO

BRINGING A MILLION DOLLAR PROJECT TO YOU – "SELL IT" BABY

The product is Dimethyl Sulforide. You can find out about this product it Chapter 5*** Million Dollar Projects - DMSO.

Is a unique product that helps take away the pain for arthritic patients and now they are researching the product to help in the cure of melanoma skin cancer. Currently the product is sold in health food stores and they put aloe in the product DMSO. They don't need the aloe in the product to make it work. The aloe is in the product to raise sales. And DMSO works fine without.

Find a pharmaceutical house that will sell you gallons of DMSO at a low price. And that is all you need to get started. Buy some dark medical bottles size 4 ounce, 8 ounce, and 16 ounce. Plus some standard boxes to fit the bottles in, for shipping.

When I sold the product, I diluted that DMSO with 20% water. It was good to dilute because 100% DMSO is too strong (that is another reason why they use aloe) and it freezes at 50°. But don't put in too much water (not more than 30% water)or you lose its working ability.

I sold the bottles for $5, $10, and $20 (4oz, 8oz, and 16oz) and made after my supplies a profit of $150 per gallon.

The magazines at the supermarket checkout stand are the best for selling. A little one inch ad is good enough with point-of-sale being Visa or MasterCard. These credit card companies take the information over the phone and put your portion of the sale into your bank account. You might want to look into cure magazines to see how much their ads are and how soon they come out. It was a great business plan then and is an excellent business now. Don't forget to put labels on your bottles. A $600 ad should render you $18,000 profit based on .0001 % of the sales.

69 – REAL ESTATE COURIER

This business carries a large security bond but like I stated in # 41 the delivery man for small business shop, this business carries $1 million profit.

The documents that are carried are very private between the buyer and the seller of the home and therefore should be transferred in special security pouches or bags. The only persons that should have a combination to the pouches are the banks, mortgage companies or other lenders involved.

The only reason the seller/buyer must wait to close the deal on the house is because the banks and the lending companies involved <u>sit on the paperwork</u> so long. With a Courier Company transporting the paperwork the waiting time is cut in half.

Background and criminal checks are a <u>must</u> with the drivers you hire. You have to show the banks and the lending companies that you have taken every precaution to ensure the security of their papers or they won't take you on as a courier company.

This is big time business and the competition is very keen so don't cut any corners to get the business <u>**EVER**</u>.

70 – INTERNET AUCTIONS

<u>Keep it simple</u>. When you need is a website, a credit card company, and craigslist for advertising your website.

It might be good to start by posting an ad in the local mailer magazine and indicate that you have an auction website. Then you need to find people on your local craigslist trying to sell whatever. Ask them if they would like to auction off their items on your website. The pictures and descriptions of their selling item, let's say a boat, are then placed on your website and let the fun begin.

The same client that has the boat is selling it for $5000 you ask him how little will you go? The client says $2500. The client then gives you a "website price" of $50 for 72 hours of

Internet time. Do not place the ad on your website without the money up front first.

It is very expensive to do what E-bay does but what you can do is give out your phone number (a special option phone number) and say that the people have 72 hours to call in. Record their name, phone number, and bid.

After the 72 hours, the highest bidder gets the client's number for buying a boat (you're out of it). If there was no bid then you tell the client that no one bid on his boat and maybe he should lower his opening bid. Either way you keep the $50 for placing the ad on your auction website. If you have several auctions going, your profit will be greater.

CHAPTER 5

MILLION DOLLAR

PROJECT

Beautiful Beautiful Pictures

After I was done with the Pet Volcano and DMSO had taken most of my money, I concentrated on my janitorial business. I still had my office but I changed it into a retail store. Because of DMSO it was now called the House of Unicorn. Back in the 70s and 80s unicorns and Pegasus were very popular and I found myself taking items ON CONSIGNMENT that had a Pegasus or unicorn theme to it. This gave me a way to sell my leftover volcanoes and DMSO plus I could make some money on the consignment items.

I received in the mail a beautiful brochure about renting a space in the Coliseum in Portland, Oregon at Thanksgiving time. This was a four day event Thursday, Friday, Saturday, and Sunday. The cost was $300 for a 10' X 10' booth. They expected a crowd of

40,000 people with no cover charge. Those sponsors also said that they were going to advertise on the radio for two weeks prior to Thanksgiving. They wanted the $300 up front to reserve the space. I had a lot of bottles of DMSO and I had plenty of volcanoes to sell plus all the, on consignment items. It sounds

like a winner to me so, I gave them the money and on that Thursday, I grabbed all my things and went to the Coliseum to set-up my booth. After I had everything set-up I looked around and it looked like about 200 spaces were sold. All in all, I had a smile on my face; it looked like a profitable weekend coming up.

What a disaster. The sponsors did not advertise on the radio and they were charging a dollar for each person at the door. Instead of 40,000 would be customers, we got 4,000 people the entire weekend. All the sellers were in shock, a lot of families gave up their Thanksgiving weekend to sell their items. The parents were sitting in their booth doing nothing while the kids were running around like their heads were cut off. I had plenty of time to walk around and look at the other booths. What I could tell, there were about four sellers that were breaking even or making money that weekend. This one person had a junky item but he had a microphone to sell it. What he had was some clear pop bottles, some spray paint, and a lazy Susan. You would put the bottles on the Lazy Susan and spray paint on the bottles. It made the bottles look pretty to put flowers in. It made money because he had a microphone and people throughout the Coliseum could hear him. So you could tell that he made his $300 back.

There was another guy that was selling tree trunk furniture. Back then, tree furniture was very popular for clocks and coffee tables. He made more than his $300 because most of his beautiful items were expensive.

There was a seller that bought his booth late but he got smart, he rented out roller-skates to all the kids running around with their heads cut off. He made more than $300 just renting skates and of course, the parents of the kids were really happy that he was there to occupy the kids.

I had no problem selling my pet volcanoes and my DMSO. My products were in the news a few months back and people remember. I didn't make a profit but I did pay for my space.

The most intriguing seller was this person who sold pictures. Now they weren't just any pictures, they were beautiful pictures of animals. These were simple pictures in black, red, and blue ink on a white background. Like I said these were beautiful pictures of different animals. The most popular were unicorns and Pegasus. He also had a snow leopard and the most unique monarch butterfly. If you look close at the butterfly you could see little animals laced in the image. Some of his pictures were laminated. He also had pictures of different sizes as well as bookmarkers and other items. What was so

great was the price. The unlamented pictures were two dollars and the laminated pictures were only four dollars. He had a line of people outside his booth just waiting to buy his pictures. He had no problem making a profit. We spoke briefly inside his booth. He said that he was going to be at the craft show next week under the bridge. That next week, I waited in line for over an hour in 15° weather just to talk to him. He finally gave me the address of the motel where he was staying at and we met that evening. He had no sense of business and we became partners with just a handshake. He gave me about 200 pictures to sell at the neighborhood flea market. I was making about $1000 a week which was great money back then and still is today. He however, was making about $10,000 a week at the craft show. People were coming to him even though it was winter time just to buy the beautiful animal pictures.

This was a dream come true. I wanted to take his pictures and go all over the country selling them. I heard that in Texas there was a flea market that had an audience of about 1 million people. If I could sell the pictures there, I would have enough front money to go to places like Burlington Northern and maybe get the pictures put on sheets and pillow cases. But I needed someone to go with me so I wouldn't get robbed while doing the flea market sales. But before I could find someone to go with me, he met a beautiful woman and she was in advertising. She told him of ways that he could sell his pictures and make profits that he never dreamed of. And of course, that took me out of the picture and out of a million dollar project. ☹

CHAPTER 8

WHAT A FLOP

TELE-

MARKETING

When I had my janitorial service in Chicago, one of the companies I cleaned was a small office complex where the owners rented out office space. They gave me this big office if I would maintain their building.

Everything was like "peas and carrots" until I met these 2 tele-marketing guys. They wanted to use my phones and exchange for showing me how to create a prospectus and clean the office building every night.

I set up an investment program for entrepreneurs. These enterprising people would come- in and tell me about their company and I would write-up this prospectus (a 3 year journey of where they thought their company was going). Once it was done, I would then find investors who were willing to listen to their ideas.

This sounded like "peas and carrots" again. Not so fast. The tele-marketing guys were on my phones 24/7. The guys had not shown me how to do a prospectus and I was a young experienced janitorial business person that knew nothing about financial office management (this was way before Google). And to top it off, they were not cleaning the office building every night. So I kicked them out of my office but not before I was thrown out of the building. I not only lost my office but the investment business as well. ☹

CHAPTER 3

100 BUSINESSES YOU CAN START WITH LITTLE OR NO MONEY

71 – RE-SELLING STORAGE ITEMS

Treasurer or junk, that's what's on the line.

Storage companies about every month have an auction on units that haven't paid their rent. The company cuts the lock and lets you "just look in" the unit to see what is inside. The highest bid pays the storage company and that person gets to go inside to see just what exactly they have bought for their hard earned cash.

And of course, if you are the one that had the highest bid, then whenever you find in the storage unit is yours to resell or keep whichever way suits your fancy. In any case you will most likely need a pickup truck to haul the stuff out of their storage unit NOW.

Hopefully, you can make a profit by hosting a garage sale of your own.

The bidding is the key. The bid needs to be low enough to gain a profit but high enough to win the bid. Remember, not every unit that you bid on is going to be what you want. Choose carefully Grasshopper. Lol

72 – DESIGN HOUSES AND DESIGN LANDSCAPES

Do you like the idea of remodeling a house or re-sculpturing a front yard? Are you always coming up with new and fresh ideas? Then maybe this is your niche.

Of course, this business isn't quite as easy as it sounds. You need to be keenly aware of your

227

surroundings. You need to search out new ideas for a home and to make them your own. You need to boldly go where you have never gone before.

The kitchen should be designed for more than one person. When you take out the walls of an entire house, leave as much room as you like for the kitchen. Don't forget the bearing walls.

When you are planning a bathroom do you just think about a tub and enough room for a large person to enjoy? Why not a hot tub or a sauna with a large shower that has 2 shower heads?

In the Southwest of the country, water is a problem. A good number of homes have no lawns it is called "zero-scape". Instead of lawns they landscape the yards with P gravel and put items in their yard like cactuses, old tires, a hand plow, and an old wheelbarrow.

Instead of a ceramic tile living room why not a step-down pit area that you can set on with a fire pit in the center.

Think outside the box. Get a good house designing software program then go to Google and check out the million designs out there. Look at them all until your eyes pop out. ☺ lol

73 – HAVE TRUCK WILL TRAVEL – OFFICE

74 – HAVE TRUCK WILL TRAVEL - WAREHOUSE

Companies from time to time move their location either for economic reasons or for expansion. The move could be in the same city or all the way across the US. In some situations they build a new office or warehouse. If you are an over the road truck driver and you have a tractor just lying around, then this might be ideal for you. Renting a trailer is relatively easy. Getting a crew together to move an office is another story. And getting a stronger crew to move a warehouse might be a challenge. You might have to hire day laborers at both-ends, the tearing down and the setting up phase.

The very best method of transporting would be by rail. You have a tractor right. Take the tractor and pick up a rail trailer, loaded up and get another rail trailer. When you have all of the equipment and supplies loaded on rail trailers then have them travel to their destination and reverse the process. If they're only going across town, renting a trailer should do the work.

You say the good Lord hasn't given you a tractor yet. Then you can do the moving in a box truck at a smaller scale of course.

Whichever is the case, bid the job as a "per load" basis and of course by the mile.

Most offices are bag up and carry. But warehouses might need tearing down fork lift shelves. Two different types of animals, two different types of manpower, so, exercise and put your back into it.

75 - INVENTORY CREW WILL TRAVEL

Inventory machines are your biggest expense plus the development of a great crew that is efficient.

Finding inventory, work in a city is one thing. Work with a crew across the US is another. The only way to expand this business and get the confidence from companies is to have a crew that has experience to get the job done in a timely fashion.

Every company that deals was selling supplies and equipment must by law have their physical selling merchandise inventoried but if you don't look like a professional service, the company will look elsewhere to get their inventory done. Training your crew to be efficient is your one and only hurdle.

76 – TAKING IN LAUNDRY

Doing someone else's laundry is not something anyone wants to do. As a matter of fact people don't want to do their own laundry. And that is why through the years gone by this job is still pumping iron.

Cleaners are still doing the work but they are not much competition because they are few and far between.

If you put an ad in a postal mailer magazine and put out some magnetic business cards on residential cars you should find enough business to stay afloat. Remember ironing is extra.

77 - BABYSITTING

This job is always available. We have a tendency to forget this one because we think of teenagers babysitting but who babysits during the week when teams are in school?

Daycare Centers, that's who, ask any mother about day care centers and you will get the same answer, they are too expensive.

If all you want are a couple of children to watch than you are okay. But if you want more then you will need to find out all the legal status that is involved.

$20 or less is all you can charge for a child. Otherwise you may not get the job. Ask the mother to provide lunch. Find out when the mother is planning to pick up their child and plan on it. But don't be too strict if the mother is a little late. However, don't let her come in an hour late every day either.

The best way to advertise is a postal mailer magazine or Craigslist.

Converting a garage into a day care center is ideal. Otherwise you may find your house trashed every day and your family will find

PEACE – NO PEACE!

Take care of children of the same age. Some older children don't take naps and babies can be a hand full. $30 a day may seem like a high price to a mother but she will pay it because it is cheaper compared to other childcare centers especially if you provide a meal and a snack.

All that you provide can be taken off your taxes including the garage which is part of the house (400 sq. ft.). Your phone, the snacks, and part of your electric bill are also tax-deductible.

With more children comes more responsibility. Do only what you can handle.

79 – SELLING COOKIES TO BEAUTY SHOPS

In ancient times I had a cookie business. My cookies were better than Mrs. Fields or at least that is what I was told. I think they just wanted my cookies.

I lived in Anaheim, California at the time and I had a friend that worked at Anaheim Stadium and she would take my cookie dough and put them in their convection ovens. The next process was wrapping the 3 inch round cookies in cellophane and putting 20 of them in a small fish tank jar.

Women love cookies. Everyone loves cookies. Anyway, I would take the fish jars to beauty salons and sell them for a dollar a piece. The beauty shops love it. The women love it. I loved it. About every 2 to 3 days I would bring a replacement fish tank jar and removal the old fish jar. The cookies were wrapped so they were good for about 10 days or more. I didn't get rich but I did make a living at it. And you can also. Just don't eat the profits. ☺ lol

80 – ERRANDS FOR PEOPLE

There are a lot of people in every neighborhood that can't get around or don't have the time or just don't want to do the errand themselves. No one likes going to the DMV, utility company, Comcast, the bank, or even to the courthouse. And who likes going to a crowded Walmart or the laundry mat as far as that goes.

You need to find these people and do their errands for them. To make it profitable you need several people with errand needs to combined the trips and save you time and gas.

It is a good business and you are doing a good service in the community. Just make sure you made a profit at the end of the day. You are like a cab without a passenger but you charge a little less to keep the customers happy.

There isn't much out-of-pocket expense you can advertise on craigslist. Plus you can do your errands at the same time.

CHAPTER 4

OUTSIDE

THE BOX

HIDDEN VALLEY

ESTATES

THIS IS NOT HOW IT HAPPENED BUT IF SOMEONE HAD BEEN THINGING OUTSIDE THE BOX, IT COULD HAVE HAPPENED THIS WAY.

Let me take you back to a similar time near Reno Nevada. When they had a small airport were just maybe six or seven flights a day. Not like it is now with an international airport and flights going out every few minutes. Let me take you just about 5 miles outside of a small Reno town back when their only was some tumbling weeds and a jackrabbit or two.

On a large hilltop, just 5 short miles overlooking a casino town with twinkling lights, A guy rides up in his car (you thought I was going to say a horse). Anyway, he drives up to this large hillside in his car and in visions something that no one else has. He says to himself; that town in the distance with all those twinkling lights is growing. This large hillside would be ideal for houses with a view of all those twinkling lights.

This land being a desert was probably about $1-$5 an acre back then. After buying up about 1000 or more acres, this land developer started thinking further. What if I section off the land in 1/3 acres for homes and have one road leading in or out of the large hillside. This will make it exclusive and secure. And what if I start to develop a golf course at the base of the hill and make it so all the homeowners on my hillside would become members of this country club golf course.

Now the property becomes an exclusive estate. All you need are just a few buyers at say $40,000 for a third acre home site and you are on your way plowing up roads and leveling off the golf course with their money. You sit back and wait for more buyers to come in to line your pockets. Now you take the golf course and sell it to the city of Reno to develop.

So for less than $5000 out-of-pocket expense he turns a profit into over $1 million and some change.

It didn't happen that way but with a little vision and thinking outside the box, it could have. WOW!

CHAPTER 7

HELPFUL HINTS

KNOW YOUR

LIMITATIONS

What are your limitations?

When I had my commercial janitorial service in Chicago, I also had a residential janitorial service at the same time. That meant that I was working during the day and late at night.

Someone made a study on sleeping habits. In that study they found that when people sleep, we sleep in cycles: light sleep, heavy sleep, dreaming, and a light sleep again. This takes about 45 minutes and then we do it all over again. When we wake up groggy that meant we woke up during our heavy sleep cycle. And when we were wake up refreshed it was because we woke up during our light sleep cycle. The study went on to say, that are best sleep was 4 ½ hours or six hour sleep cycles and six hours or eight hour sleep cycles. There has been a ton of more studies just like all the hundreds of studies on dieting.

Anyway, I followed this study and found I did best after 4 ½ hours of rest. And that worked great for my lifestyle of working day and night.

Still I didn't push myself. If the work called or two people like when I was stripping and waxing floors, I got a second person. And when I took on more ventures like my tax business, I watch to make sure it wasn't too much. It is great to make the money but if you don't have the time to spend it, what good as it?

In Reno, Nevada I started up my painting business again. I also did repairs and handyman work. I thought of being a property manager because I was doing all of the skills but I want to make sure, so I took 2 short courses in real estate and got certified as a property manager. I get the same thing when I wanted to do my own taxes for my janitorial business. I spent $350 and took a tax course with H&R Block. When I want to be a bartender in Reno Nevada I went to a bartending school.

Don't think you know the work. **MAKE SURE!** Working for a painting business will give you the skills for starting your own painting business.

Whatever you do, don't do what I did. I sacrificed my family over having a business. In my case, it was working day and night and never taking enough time for my family. I understand that you need to start your own business. It is an "itch" that has to be scratched or you'll go nuts. But understand **ALL** not just a few but **ALL** new businesses take 10 to 14 hours a day to make them work. Just know your priorities and make quality time with your family.

CHAPTER 3

100 BUSINESSES
YOU CAN START
WITH
LITTLE OR NO
MONEY

81 – COMMERCIAL CARPET CLEANING SERVICE

This business is very similar to #52 - Residential Carpet Cleaning Service except there are a lot more furniture and a lot more carpets to be cleaned. Plus, a lot more cash in your pocket. But in the same token, you will need a lot more equipment and a few more employees to get the job done. Uniforms are a must with your logo on them to give you that professional look.

When you are giving a bid to the company set up a provision that you come back every three or four months.

The job should be planned on the weekend so the carpet had a chance to dry. And you will need to be bonded so you can have a set of keys. Otherwise you will be locked in. Don't forget the coasters for the furniture legs.

82 – VALET PARKING

Some parts of the country do not know what valet parking is. Simply, it is taking someone's car at the time when they are getting out and parking it for them.

At someone's home they might be having a wedding reception or maybe a party if they don't have the room for cars they can call in your services.

Now find a place really close by where you can park the car and run back to grab another car. The best way, is to have someone with a car at the lot where the cars are being parked and they can bring you back to the party. When the guest leaves, phone down to have their car brought up.

There are a few nice wrinkles to this service. You can offer this service to a lot at a football game or any place where people are gathering like at a grand opening.

A different twist would be at that same lot for the football game, offer to take the people from a lot to the game and back when the game is over.

LOTS OF TIPS ☺

83 – HOUSE BARTENDING

I mentioned earlier that I went to Bartending School in Reno, Nevada. My instructor found me a job in a huge casino. I started out in the lowest position in a showroom behind the scenes. But in four short months I was one of four head bartenders and known for my frozen margaritas. I made (back then) $35 a night but my tips were over $100 a night. I drove a Camaro with wide track. Smooth! I drove that car until it got repossessed because I lost my job January 1st the day after <u>New Year's Eve.</u> That night we were on speed dial in portable bars with 15,000 crazy people around us waiting for the Canon to go off at midnight. My friends told me a month earlier, that the owner of the casino normally gets rid of his head bartenders New Year's Day only to be replaced by bar-backs who don't know how to pour one drink let-alone 140 drinks. They were right. January 1st, I was out of a job.

The first 90 days of a new year are the slowest profit days anywhere and especially in Reno, Nevada. I couldn't find a job nowhere in town doing anything. And bartending jobs if there was one were going to women with large bra sizes if you know what I mean.

Home bartending is a different story. Go to the library and check out the latest books on mixing drinks. Memorize as many or all of them. Then if you can practice with colored water, ice, and garnishes like lemon peel.

Get a vest, a white long sleeved shirt, and a bow-tie so you look the part. Place an ad in a postal mailer magazine and you should be all set. Oh! Don't forget to smile and maybe you'll get a tip. ☺

84 – SIT DOWN DATING SERVICE

Have you ever seen a sit down dating service? I have seen them on TV but never a person, not that I am looking. I'm too old for that sort of thing. But it seems like the best way to meet someone rather than over the Internet.

What you need to do first is to find a place that will let you work your magic once or twice a week. The most ideal place would be a restaurant/bar that isn't too busy during the week in the early evening say from 6 to 7 PM or 7to 8 PM. Try to locate several places in different parts of the city maybe even different days of the week.

Place an ad in a postal mailer magazine. What I would do is have the people make reservations with you so you know how many men and how many women are going to show up. Ask them over the phone, what day of the week they would like to go and give them a place and a time. Try to get their first name and phone number just in case there is a cancellation because the response is too low. The trickiest part is giving them a price. You can start out at ten dollars a person but it may not be enough or maybe the price for women needs to be less. Everything depends on the restaurant owner and the response from the advertisement. After a few weeks you should have no problem getting enough people to participate in your program. Maybe you can give the restaurant owner some fliers to pass out to some of his customers during the week.

Set aside about the space of no more than six tables at each location. Each location will have 2 chairs per table and a bell or dinger. Plus a 3 minute egg timer. Now you are all set. Happy hunting. ☺

85 – TERM PAPERS

Prerequisite – You need to know how to type well and how to read scribble. Lol

This is always a good business around college campuses especially close to midterm. Spring for some business cards and pass them out around campus.

THAT'S IT!

I would think that your price would be based on words and any other criteria that may need to be done with the paper. And of course, the more clients you have the more money you make as long as you can meet their deadlines.

86 – PET SITTING/PLANT SITTING

People need to take a vacation but they can't always take their pets and they sure can't take their plants.

Animals need more than food and water. Their shepherd (owner) just went across the earth and fell off. Who is going to take care of us? They have been gone for an hour. Are they ever coming back? And who are you?

As a pet sitter it would be a wise move to get to know the pet before the owner leaves. Plus you need to know their habits, their food, and their vet just in case.

You won't be staying overnight but you should visit the pets at least twice a day to reassure them that there is a friend around who can feed us, walk us, and pet us a lot.

Plants and lawn sitting is less emotional but they need TLC also. It wouldn't hurt to talk to the plants when you're watering them. My plants like to be touched too.

Don't over water me. Now go away your blocking the sun. Thank You! Oh! Come back as soon as you can.

87 – HOUSE SITTING

Sitting at someone else's house needs some respect they are having you stay for a few hours a night or overnight for whatever reason "so the house looks like someone is home". Respect it!

Every time you enter the house you should check to see if the windows and doors are locked. Don't just look but check it out. Make sure everything is in its place. Turning on the lights and walking is also part of the job. You need to have emergency numbers just in case you have a question.

It is not wise to have a friend over unless the owners have approved the idea ahead of time. Relax and read a book or watch TV. I wouldn't watch anything scary. Lol

88 – RESIDENTIAL PAINTING

You need experience for this line of work or you could screw-up the owner's house. There is one thing to paint your own kitchen, it's different to paint someone else's kitchen especially for money.

The owner is going to want a professional job for his money. That means cleaning any grease on the walls, drop clothes on the floor and/or furniture, using quality paint, patching any holes, and most of all running a straight line trim. **YOU NEED TO BE EXPERIENCED ***** DON'T BE STUPID**

Work for a painting company for about a year before you tackling a job on your own. One, it will give you the experience you need and two, you will have a better understanding on how to bid and not lose your shorts in the process.

NO SHORT CUTS

Some painters try to cheat again to use shortcuts to save a buck. Pressure washing is <u>always</u> needed for painting the outside of the house. Holes <u>always</u> need to be patched. If you paint over the holes, the paint will dry and the holes may come back. Cleaning greasy walls is a must. Paint does not stick to grease. Using Kilz on the wall will save you hours and a lot of paint if the wall bleeds back.

Don't use cheap paint it will cost you more in the long run. And use a drop cloth. The moment you don't use a drop cloth is the moment you wish you did. There is nothing worse than stepping in paint and tracking it all over the house.

Painters should look professional. White shirt, white pants, a white hat and only buy professional equipment and supplies. Good professional brushes (which are very expensive) will give you that professional quality you should have. Once you have spent the money you will **NEVER** go back to cheap again.

Don't drag about a job. You will begin to hate the job and the owner will get disappointed.

Work from top to bottom

Work from walls to trim

Work from flat to semi-gloss

(Semi-gloss will cover flat but flat will not cover semi-gloss)

When you are bidding, only include the labor. You can make a guess on the paint and supplies. Example: the labor for the house inside is $2000. The paint is about 1 gallon for every room so if you have 18 months that would be (4) 5 gallon drums of paint (the price of (3) 1 gallon cans is equal to a 5 gallon drum of paint). Thinking that the paint cost $100 per drum I would say it like this: my labor is $2000 and the paint probably will cost about $500. I will require one third of the labor cost up front and the cost of the paint. <u>Non-negotiable,</u> If they don't agree, **SAY NOTHING**, turn around and leave. PERIOD, If you cave-in you will lose money and respect. Also if you cave-in the owner will tell his friends and you will have to cave-in with them as well.

DON'T CAVE-IN ON PRICE

One more thing, when you get the paint don't let a <u>moron</u> mix it for you. Insist on a person who knows what they are doing. Don't ever go to Walmart for any paint needs. The products are cheap and no one works in the paint department. They are an inexperienced because they come from different departments and they are just filling in.

Also don't let the owner get the paint. He doesn't have the experience to be on his own and he may choose cheap paint. It is okay not to listen to me. If it happens once, you won't let it happen again.

89 – ENTREPRENEUR BUSINESS

In my "What a Flop" – telemarketing, I explained about this business. It can be very rewarding if the business is done well. But it takes a few investment dollars to make it work.

No one is going to come to you with their inventions if you don't look and act successful. What you need is a nice office with nice furniture but nothing too fancy. You need a median priced suit. The secretary would be good although there is nothing for her to do except greet the clients.

What you are doing is greeting the clients and listening to their stories as to why they need money. It is like Shark Tank except your client has no proven profit record. Next is making a prospectus portfolio for the client for which you charge them about $500. This portfolio mentions what the business is and what a three year projection would look like if they had some investment capital to work with. Next, you set up a special presentation room with all the props and lots of comfortable chairs that look alike. You need a computer with a large TV screen monitor and a table with copies of the portfolios for every investor to look at.

The investors should be easy to find on craigslist. The investors need to call for an appointment so you will know exactly how many people are going to show up that way you can be prepared for their coming.

What you have a few people coming for the showing. You need to do the presentation yourself to the investors and not the client giving the presentation.

1% of the investment or 1% of the company's business profit should be given to you. You need to decide before giving the presentation.

90 – COMPUTER AUCTION BUYING/SELLING

In most large cities there are computer auctions. We have them twice a year here. All of the schools and offices upgrade their computers every few years and they have an auction companies selling their old computers at the highest bidder.

What you do in turn is get the winning bid on these computers, change out the hard drive and put an operating system on them like

Windows 8 and then resell the computers at a profit. These computers can be bought for less than $.50 on the dollar. And Microsoft will give you a special deal on operating systems if you buy 10 at a time. PIRATING AN OPERATING SYSTEM IS ILLEGAL AND COULD COME BACK TO HAUNT YOU. If you don't know much about computers find somebody who does that is willing to help you. But have an <u>Eagle eye</u> on them to make sure they don't rip you off or do something illegal.

Sometimes you can find someone was selling 10 computers at a discount on craigslist. It might be good to ask why they are selling so many computers at one time. (Eagle eye)

Craigslist or flea markets are an excellent way to sell your finished computers.

CHAPTER 5

MILLION DOLLAR

PROJECT

KROO POCKETS

Long time ago before the earth was formed. No; not quite that long ago. Anyway, I had these Christian friends and we had a designing product. It was revolutionary at the time. The three of us were trying real hard to get this product off the ground. One of the guys came up with the idea. I took his idea and designed several uses for the products. The third guy had a little money but we all had the Lord and we prayed about it a lot. ☺

Whenever you are producing a product there is a lot of "leg work". Those of you that have designed a product in the past know what I'm talking about. You design something and then you have a prototype made-up to see what it looks like. You get a prototype made you have to find a manufacturer that is willing to "tool" (die-cut) your design. The cost is <u>crazy</u>. For about 50 to 100 times more than the finished product would cost to the public. The product was good on paper but until you have it in your hand you have no idea what you have produced. It took us several prototypes before we had the product we were looking for, Kroo Pockets.

Like I said in the beginning our product was revolutionary at the time. The product was made from the same material used on backpacks and gym bags today. Our product had Velcro and each idea had a pocket like a kangaroo.

Everything was like peas and carrots until we had to manufacture the product. You have the work done in the states it would cost the same amount that we were going to sell the product for to the public. So our profit margin would be nothing. We found a manufacturer in China that can reproduce our product for about 1% of the retail price. I know, China, not exactly made in the USA. It was the shipping that ended up being the problem. The cost for shipping each item wasn't bad at all but we had to ship 100,000 items in a container at a time which made the total cost about $30,000 (which was like $300,000 today). We didn't have the money so we had to scrap the idea. ☹

CHAPTER 11

ESTIMATING

THE COST

So you think you know how to paint a house.

So you think you know how to clean an office.

So you think you know how to cut a lawn.

So you think you know how to build a deck.

So you think you know how to do whatever. But do you know how to estimate? You can pick-up from the library a book on how to estimate and by reading it thoroughly you might discover how to estimate the cost of building a bridge.

I remember one time estimating the cost of janitorial cleaning of the 10 office buildings for Union Pacific. They had companies like me competing for the job. One guy had a measuring wheel. As he walked along the measuring wheel would measure the length of each room. That guy didn't get the job, he was too busy measuring the room and not paying attention to details. I got the job for several reasons. When I was looking over the rooms, I guess-ti-mated their size and how much attention that room needed to do the cleaning. A good rule of thumb (most of that time) is to have a general idea how a company thinks when it comes to bidding. If you have 5 bids don't be the highest bid. Companies really don't want to spend all their profits on you. Don't be the lowest bid. The company may thing you are too hungry for the work and may not be any good. Plus it is not good to under bid and eat up all your profits. No, the best bid placement is second from the bottom of the bid scale. The company will think you are not out to gouge them and they can save money with you doing the work.

Actually, one of the main reasons why I got the job was when I talked to the owner of the company and shook his hand with confidence. His hand was sweating and I knew at that moment I had the job over the competition because I acted like I had experience to get the task done. That made my bid spot on.

Multi-graphics was another story. 900,000 ft.^{2} and they wanted $100,000 bond ($10,000 real money). I couldn't afford it so they let me bid on their 25 restrooms that were to be cleaned three times a day.

Max Factor was too flamboyant. They didn't know when they wanted a janitorial service or what they wanted cleaned. Their head was in the clouds most of the time because they were high scale advertising six months in advance to stay ahead of their competition.

The worst company I ever dealt with was a real estate company that put a special clause in the bidding contract. It stated: while the job is underway, if there is additional work to be done it will be included in the original price with no increase.

When you submit a bid and they rewrite the proposal, make sure you read every line before signing.

When making a bid for a job consider how long the job is going to take? What materials are you going to need? Are you going to need help? What is your travel time and gas? And are you free to do the job the way you want?

Food stores are notorious for locking you in. That is like tying your hands. If you need something or if there is an emergency, forget it, you are locked in.

Beauty salons and barbershops are the easiest job is to get in a janitorial business. It is the hair on the floor that gets you into trouble. Once you use a mop on that floor you can't use that mop again **EVER**.

In the janitorial business the childcare centers are the best jobs for the money. They are required by law to keep the place clean every day. It's a lot of work though, stripping floors and shampooing carpets but it is great money.

Commercial janitorial work is one of the least out-of-pocket businesses to start. A vacuum, mop N bucket, a duster, trash bags, and some cleaning supplies are pretty much all you need.

I always started the regular service with a one-time job like stripping floors or shampooing carpets. You can rent a stripping machine which can double as a shampooer for carpets. Later on you can watch on Craigslist for a stripping machine on sale.

Advertising to a company to get their cleaning business is easy as pie too. You send a letter or a black and white brochure explaining about your janitorial service. You don't have to go into too much detail. If they need your service, they will call. If they don't need your janitorial service at this time they will deep six your letter no matter how nice it is because they won't even look at it.

In the beginning, you will over think your bid but that is not a bad thing. What is bad, is when you under think your bid. It takes practice and experience to bid right. I used to get 80% of my bids for the jobs. When you're trying to get 80% be careful and don't lose your shirt. It is going to happen, so just buy another shirt and move on. Good Luck. ☺

CHAPTER 3

100 BUSINESSES

YOU CAN START

WITH

LITTLE OR NO

MONEY

91 – FLEA MARKET COMPUTERS

I did this for a living once and a handsome living it was.

Competition will be keen. What you need are flat screens for your computer and a reasonable price for the customer while still making a profit for yourself.

You lure the customer to your booth by showing movies on your computers. You will also need speakers to go with the computers.

Whatever you do don't let kids touch your computers. They know how to disrupt your programs. As a matter of fact, it is best if the computers are handled by you alone. PERIOD

I always made an attractive setting for my computer by putting a small table on top of a large table and using a beautiful cloth over the table. A cloth can be bought at Walmart in their fabric department. With computers at different levels it made for a special setting when people were walking by.

Request a booth along the main aisle but away from others selling computers.

The movie, "When Harry Met Sally" and Meg Ryan demonstrates in a restaurant her orgasm sounds, it was priceless for selling computers. ☺

92 – FLEA MARKET MISC.

Understand flea markets are great for making some cash now. But you have to look at the customers from the outside looking in. They have literally hundreds of thousands of different items to look at and the customer may be limited with the cash they can spend and that is if they want to spend money at all. When you are going fishing you use the best bait possible to lure the fish in. I am not saying that customers are fish what I am saying, if you want the customers to come over to your booth, you need some bait.

HOW CAN YOU WIN THE WORLD IF NOBODY KNOWS YOU'RE THERE?

First you need a beautiful display. On Fifth Avenue of New York City the most expensive shops all have beautiful displays. Yes you will need to create a want. Remember, they may not even be there at the flea market to buy anything. Maybe a discount will spark some life in them. Or how about: "This week only!" Another good one is: "The last 5 left".

It wouldn't hurt the sale if <u>you</u> look nice and not sloppy. And saying hello doesn't hurt either. But if you're sitting back reading a book the only thing that will get done all day is maybe a chapter in that book.

Don't sell junk at a flea market. Sell junk at a garage sale.

BRINGING A

MILLION DOLLAR PROJECT TO YOU

The product is material used for gym bags and back packs plus the use of Velcro for the pockets.

The product was unique when we were planning it together. That's why only China could handle keeping the price low enough to make a profit. But now, I'm sure that there are American manufacturers that could handle it nicely.

Grant you, there are a few different items out there but I haven't seen that many compared to the 40 different items we came up with. The chair saddlebag for magazines comes to mind. You take a chair on the beach or at home and connect the saddlebag over the arm or the back of the chair. A small pocket for a house key on a belt is a nice touch. A saddlebag with pockets for your dog is very handy to put your phone or a book when going to the park. A ball cap with a small pocket for a house key so you don't get locked out of the house works fine. A tree wrap with a warm liner for the hard freeze winter with a small pocket for a thermometer and/or a bungee cord. A small plant wrap with a pocket for thermometer and/or a bungee cord.

These are just a few items. Be creative. **WIPE OUT** the competition with wild new designs on the material. This is a doable business and if you don't do it, someone else will.

94 – COMPUTER WAREHOUSING

There are millions and millions of items being sold on the computer every day. Spend a lot of time checking out websites till your eyes bug out ☺ and you will find that it will be time well spent.

You will need a website of your own. There is strength in numbers, put thousands of items on your website plus a <u>search item</u> plug. You will be surprised at the hits you will achieve from somebody else's items. You will also need a cashier's area and a place to put credit card numbers, customer names, addresses, and phone numbers of the customer.

You can advertise on Craigslist in different parts of the United States with your website as a key ingredient. Don't use your phone number, email or your personal address in the advertisement. Just your website address is all you need.

Your site should be secure and let the customers know that feature. There are also credit card companies that you can call in the customer number and the money will go to your account minus a small fee of course. Pay Pal is an excellent source as well.

Have the items that the customer wants to buy from your website shipped from the original owner's website to the customer directly if at all possible. Sometimes if the item is cheap, the profit will be made in the shipping and handling.

95 – COMPUTER LINKING

People are making millions just computer linking. If you have a website on your computer then all you need to do is have people who surf on to your website go to other websites via your link.

You need to connect with the different websites and asked for a link. They will give you a link with a counter on it. Everyone who uses your link to get onto their webpage the website will pay you about $.10 each. Not much but those dimes can add up if you have 100 links or more.

96 – COMPUTER SOFT LINKING

This one is really good. When you set up a website, have the provider give you as many pages as you want. Put whatever you want on your website and have links to other pages on your site and sell the monthly spaces to your friends or others who don't have a website but they have a business that they would like to promote. If you get enough monthly subscribers, they will not only pay for your website but they can also give you some pocket change as well. And all you have to do is design a "picture page" for your friends with their phone number and maybe their address.

97 – CRAIGLIST SELLING

This is a great way to sell your personal items. You can sell them where you live or across the

US. Just use a lot of pictures. No one buys anything without a picture. **TRUST ME.**

Once you have established your ad with different wording for three days, you can place your ad every day with just a click of a few buttons.

If you want to expand, the start selling other people's items on Craigslist as well.

98 – LOCAL BOOKKEEPING/TAX BUSINESS

You need to know how to do bookkeeping and taxes. Read chapter 9 & 10.

Taxes are easy and life supporting, I did it for 40 years. I added bookkeeping to my business because it was easier on Quicken Books to take the bottom line of the profit and loss statement and apply it to the taxes. Also the bookkeeping business got me more tax customers.

You don't have to learn how to do taxes if you do TurboTax online. Just have the customer pay for any fees online without telling them that you're doing it on TurboTax. If they know you are doing their taxes on TurboTax they will say; forget you, I will do it on TurboTax myself.

I prefer to do taxes on paper from the IRS.gov/forms. I can do any easy tax in less than 10 minutes and TurboTax takes an hour to do the same taxes. I used TurboTax only when I am e-filing a return or if there are special taxes like Corporation taxes.

I never had competition because I set-up an office on a busy street with no other tax offices near my office. My prices were low and I always gave my price over the phone. 90% of all tax places will not give you any price over the phone. H&R Block and many others will have you wait in a line for over an hour before giving you the bad news of how much the cost will be. It makes the customer want to leave and go to another tax place but instead they pay the price because if they leave they will just have to go to another tax place that will have them waiting in line again before they find out how much they charge.

I never had my clients wait in line at all (only if they wanted to). They would drop off their forms and pick up a finished copy the following day.

Try to get the money up front. If the customer owes taxes they may want to stiff you. **NO CHECKS EVER** just cash or credit cards.

99 – INTERNET TAXES

100 – INTERNET BOOKKEEPING

Both businesses can be done together or separate it depends on you. Chapter 10 on taxes and #98 – Local Bookkeeping and Tax Business and read chapter 8 on bookkeeping.

Both businesses have the same scenarios, Craigslist for your website only throughout the US.

Show on your website all you can do for them. Printed forms can be sent to their email account as an attachment. Get your money up front first or the work will be done for free. Duh!

TurboTax online and a cheap Quicken Books DVD program are all you'll need for these businesses. Expect a large volume of business especially if you keep your prices low and have a secure website that the customer knows about. **ALL THEIR INFORMATION IS CONFIDENTIAL. RIGHT!**

CHAPTER 7

HELPFUL HINTS

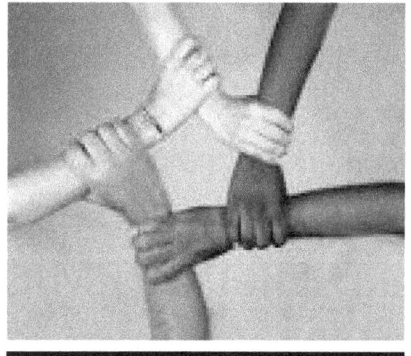

COMBINE

BUSINESSES

Combining the work you do can only increase your revenue but too much work may BOG you down. Out of the 100 businesses I have combined a few that might work together well.

21 & 22 – Maid & Butler Service Referrals

24 & 25 – Residential & Commercial Handyman Services

33, 34, & 35 - Doctor, Dentist, & Lawyer Referral Services

The last three are what I was referring to when I said; the work might be too much what with all the data that has to be accumulated.

52 & 81 – Residential & Commercial Carpet Cleaning Services

The one thing about getting BOGGED down with combining businesses; it can ruin the one business you are trying to start.

55, 56, & 57 – Porch and Deck Designing, Building, & Painting

There is another problem with combining businesses, if you are experienced in one of the businesses but you are not in the other businesses, it isn't going to work unless you get some training, SOMEWHERE.

58 & 89 – Regular Garage Floor and Driveway Painting plus Residential Painting

59, 60, 61, & 62 – Designing Trips for Big & Small Churches, Companies, and People

Now these jobs 59, 60, 61, & 62 are ideal for each other. All the information you gather-up can be used for each of the other businesses.

64 & 65 – Garage Sales and Master Garage Selling

73 & 74 – Moving Crew will Travel – Office & Warehouse

76 & 77 – Taking in laundry & Baby Sitting

87 & 88 – Dog Sitting/Plant Sitting & House Sitting

99 & 100 – Internet Tax & Bookkeeping Services

CHAPTER 12

RETIRED

I'm retired now or as retired as one can be in this economy. I still do taxes and a little painting on the side. Anyway, being semi-retired I wanted to write this book to inspire people like yourself and not to be afraid of starting your own business. I hope you won't be like so many others before you, forgeting business cards and throw yourselves to the wind. Think about the business you are about to start. Try to improve on it every day. If you forget yourself and just think about the customer's needs you will find yourself saying, as I did, "What competition?"

Owning your own business gives you the freedom to discipline yourself and basically answer to no one, completely independent from the world.

NOW THAT IS RETIREMENT IN ITS PUREST FORM

royaldyman@gmail.com

www.ingramcontent.com/pod-product-compliance
Lightning Source LLC
Chambersburg PA
CBHW051629170526
45167CB00001B/115